INTROVERT'S

SOUTHERN UTAH

Travel for Crowd Haters

How to Avoid Crowds While Traveling

Linus Alden Knight

CONTENTS

INTRODUCTION

"There is nothing like the thrill of arriving in a landscape so magnificent and vast, only to discover you have it all to yourself." - Anonymously Introverted.

Welcome to Southern Utah, an introvert's dream where solitude and scenery embrace a breathtaking spectacle.

Southern Utah is an anomaly of sorts, offering both boundless beauty and ample room to breathe. This stark, rugged part of the American Southwest is where introverts can wander through landscapes that look more like Mars than Earth without bumping into selfie sticks at every turn. Here, the red rocks soar into the sky, the canyons plunge into the abyss, and the vast skies stretch into eternity, painted with the hues of an artist's palette.

This guide, "Introvert's Southern Utah Travel for Crowd Haters," is crafted for those who find joy in the quiet corners of the world, for those who revel in the art of being alone without being lonely, and for travelers who want to experience nature's wonders up close, without the hum of a crowd in the background.

Overview of Southern Utah

Southern Utah is home to some of the most iconic national parks in the United States, including Zion, Bryce Canyon, Capitol Reef, Arches, and Canyonlands. Each park offers unique geological formations and awe-inspiring landscapes that attract millions of visitors annually. Yet, despite their popularity, there are still untold stories written in the quiet nooks and secret vistas far from the well-trodden paths.

The region extends from the lush, high plateaus of the Dixie National Forest to the stark, stony whispers of Monument Valley. It's a land where history is written in the stratified cliffs and ancient ruins and where the horizon tempts with endless adventures.

Importance of Crowd Avoidance for a More Enjoyable Experience

For the introvert traveler, crowd avoidance is not just a preference—it's essential for enjoying the journey. Crowds can transform a serene hike into a bustling queue, a peaceful sunrise into a chaotic photo op, and a quiet moment of reflection into a cacophony of voices. In Southern Utah, the magic lies in the isolated moments, where the only sounds are the wind's whisper and your footsteps.

Finding solitude here is about comfort and connection. It's about experiencing the primal beauty of nature without a filter, connecting with the land on a personal level, and letting the quiet majesty of the desert inspire peace and introspection.

Brief on What the Book Will Cover

This book is your quiet companion through the rugged heart of the Southwest. It will guide you to the hidden gems and less-visited corners of Southern Utah's national parks. Expect to explore:

- **Secret Trails and Times:** Learn when to visit popular spots when they're least crowded, and discover trails where you can walk for hours without seeing another soul.

- **Solitude in Scenic Spots:** Uncover scenic lookouts and serene spots that offer stunning views without the crowds.

- **Introvert-Friendly Itineraries:** Tailor-made itineraries that prioritize peace over popularity, allowing you to explore at your own pace.

- **Tips for Quiet Travel:** From the best times to travel and how to avoid peak seasons to the art of stealth camping and finding tranquility even in the most visited parks.

"Introvert's Southern Utah Travel for Crowd Haters" promises to be more than just a travel guide; it's a passage to personal discovery amidst some of the planet's most spectacular scenery.

CHAPTER 1

Planning Your Trip

Starting a journey to Southern Utah is similar to preparing for a visit to another planet, except, thankfully, you can leave your space suit at home, and there's no need to worry about zero-gravity toilets. That said, planning a trip where the main itinerary includes avoiding other human beings as much as the sights themselves does require a certain fine touch and a strategic mastermind.

Firstly, timing is everything. Visit during the shoulder seasons—late spring or early autumn—to dodge the deluge of families freed from the shackles of the school calendar and sun-seekers hoping to sizzle under the desert sun. You'll find the weather during these times is as pleasant as a warm cup of tea on a rainy afternoon—comfortable enough for hiking yet cool enough to keep the crowds at bay.

Accommodation is your next strategic play. While one might think camping under the stars is an introvert's paradise, remember that popular campgrounds can resemble rock festivals minus the music. Opt instead for lesser-known campgrounds or consider a charming bed and breakfast where the only breakfast companion you might encounter is a quietly curious chipmunk.

Finally, arm yourself with a map that shows the paths and the beaten paths. The kind of maps that reveal secret trails and solitary landscapes, the kind that local rangers whisper about and only divulge if you promise to leave no trace.

Choosing the Right Time to Visit

Ah, the perennial challenge for the introverted traveler: when to visit Southern Utah to experience its vast expanses without the pesky interference of other human beings. It's a delicate balance, like choosing the right ripeness of a banana. Too early, and you're donning layers like an onion; too late, and you might just melt into a human puddle under the relentless desert sun.

Let's dissect the problem of timing your visit, examine the off-peak versus peak seasons, and consider the whims of weather.

Off-Peak Seasons vs. Peak Seasons

Venturing into Southern Utah during the off-peak seasons is a bit like attending a blockbuster movie during a weekday matinee — you might just get the whole place to yourself. The peak seasons, from late spring to early fall, lure crowds akin to bees on honey due to school holidays and the siren call of summer vacations. If you find solace in solitude, aim for the edges of these times.

Spring (March to May) starts k and shyly warms up, while fall (September to November) begins with the remnants of summer heat before chilling into sweater weather. These transitional periods offer mild temperatures and present Southern Utah in varying palettes — vibrant spring blooms or the fiery foliage of fall. Here, the secret is to target the very start or end of these seasons. Think of late March when the chill is just leaving the air or late October when the crowds have receded but the trees are still showing off their autumnal hues.

Weather Considerations

When planning your travel based on weather, it's important to remember that Southern Utah is a region of microclimates, each with its temperamental weather patterns. Elevations vary wildly, from the valley floors to the towering cliffs, and with them, temperatures can swing. Mornings can be crisp enough to see your breath, while afternoons might call for sunscreen and a hat. Checking historical weather patterns can be as crucial as packing the right shoes.

- **Spring** brings temperate days, but the nights can be cold, often dipping below freezing in higher elevations like Bryce Canyon, which sits regally at over 8,000 feet. This is a time for wildflowers and melting snow, for waterfalls briefly fattened by the runoff, offering dramatic backdrops for the solitary wanderer.

- **Summer** transforms the landscape into a sunbaked oven, especially in lower areas like Zion Canyon, where temperatures can soar to over 100 degrees Fahrenheit. While summer is the peak of the peak season, there's a trick to beating both the heat and the crowds: start your hikes at dawn. Not only will you witness some of the most stunning sunrises, but you'll also have the trails largely to yourself as most tourists are less inclined to rise with the sun.

- **Fall** is perhaps the Goldilocks season for visiting Southern Utah. The weather cools down, making outdoor adventures during the day utterly pleasant, and the evenings are perfect for cozy campfires. The changing leaves against the backdrop of red rock canyons provide a spectacular display of nature's artistry. Plus, the decrease in visitor numbers during this season means you can enjoy the tranquility that comes with lesser foot traffic.

- **Winter** is the unsung hero of seasons for those truly committed to avoiding other people. The cold is a deterrent for many, leaving the landscapes hauntingly beautiful and serene. Snow dusting the red rocks creates a stunning contrast, and popular spots like Arches and Canyonlands transform into quiet, stark wonderlands. Just be prepared for potential road closures and ensure you're equipped for icy conditions.

Choosing the right time to visit Southern Utah is about aligning the cosmos of your comfort with climate and crowd. Go in the fringe months of spring or fall for the best combination of solitude and scenery, and always be prepared for Mother Nature's whims. This way, your travels will be memorable and marvelously peaceful.

Duration of Stay

One might wonder how long it takes to appreciate the grand solitude of Southern Utah thoroughly. The answer, much like trying to determine how many licks it takes to get to the center of a Tootsie Pop, is wonderfully subjective. However, unlike the Tootsie Pop inquiry, which can end in a sticky mess and a profound sense of futility, planning the duration of your stay in Southern Utah can be broken down into digestible, delightful itineraries.

Suggested Itineraries for Different Trip Lengths

- **Weekend Warrior (2-3 Days):** If you're the kind of person who likes to dive deep and fast, a weekend in Southern Utah might just suffice. Start your expedition in Zion National Park. A day's hike up to Angels Landing offers breathtaking views and a satisfying challenge. The next morning, make your way to Bryce Canyon for a brisk walk along the Rim Trail, enjoying the otherworldly silence that sunrise there offers. It's a quick dip into nature's majesty, but like a well-made espresso, it's short, potent, and leaves you buzzing.

- **One Week Wanderer (7 Days):** Seven days in Southern Utah allows you to explore the 'Mighty 5' National Parks without feeling like you're rushing through your vacation. Begin at Arches National Park, spending a couple of days marveling at its over 2,000 natural stone arches. Midweek, head to Canyonlands for a day of quiet contemplation by the Mesa Arch – early morning visitation can feel like having a private viewing. Round off your week with visits to Capitol Reef, Bryce, and Zion. Each park is a chapter in a novel you can't put down, full of plot twists in the form of sudden canyons and dramatic vistas.

- **Two Weeks or More (14+ Days):** For the truly dedicated, a fortnight or longer allows full immersion into the solitude and splendor of Southern Utah. With more time, you can add day-long hikes or even multi-day backcountry adventures in each park. Consider delving into the lesser-known parts of each park to find true solitude. Include a day or two in the nearby state parks like Goblin Valley—a haven for those who prefer their landscapes beautifully bizarre. With more days at your disposal, you can afford to wake up with no plan other than to drive until something magnificent stops you. That's the luxury of time.

Budgeting for Your Trip

Budgeting for a trip to Southern Utah is somewhat akin to preparing for a small expedition. You're not just accounting for meals and accommodations; you're planning for an adventure. Here's how to ensure your finances remain as calm as the deserted trails you seek.

Cost Considerations for Lodging, Food, and Activities

- **Lodging:** Lodging in Southern Utah ranges from the dirt-cheap (literally, if you're camping) to the delightful luxe. Campsites in the national parks are affordable but need to be booked well in advance, especially during peak seasons. They can run from $15 to $50 per night, depending on the location and facilities. For more comfort, local motels and hotels can vary from $50 to upwards of $200 per night. The key here is to book early; last-minute deals are as rare as a quiet moment in Times Square on New Year's Eve.

- **Food:** If you're out on the trails, you'll be packing most of your meals. Local grocery stores have a variety of provisions that will keep the bank intact. Plan to spend around $10-$15 per day on food if you self-cater. Dining out, however, can add a bit more. Restaurants in tourist-heavy areas know their audience well and price accordingly. A meal out can range from $15 to $30 per person, not including the tip. My advice? Find the local diners. The food is hearty, the atmosphere is often filled with local charm, and the prices are gentler on the wallet.

- **Activities:** The major cost here will be the park entrance fees, which are $30-$35 per vehicle for a seven-day pass. If you plan to visit multiple parks, consider the America the Beautiful Pass for $80, which covers all national parks for a year. Guided tours and special activities like horseback riding or ATV tours can push your budget upwards of $100 per person. However, the beauty of Southern Utah lies in its abundance of free activities. Hiking, photography, bird watching, and stargazing cost nothing but your time and attention.

Whether you're pinching pennies or loosening the purse strings, the returns on investment are spectacular: endless vistas, profound tranquility, and the kind of joy that only comes from discovering the great outdoors on your terms.

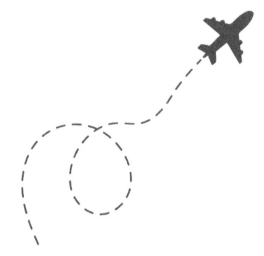

CHAPTER 2

Destinations for Crowd Haters

Southern Utah, with its sprawling red rock vistas and sky-piercing spires, is a magnet for those with cameras, hiking boots, and a yearning for the grandeur of the great outdoors. Yet, for every crowded viewpoint and bustling trailhead, myriad hidden gems remain blissfully overlooked by the tourist crowds.

Hidden Gems in Southern Utah

Venturing off the beaten path in Southern Utah is like flipping to the less-read pages of your favorite book—familiar yet wholly surprising. Here are several clandestine locales where you can relish the grandiosity of nature without the din of crowds:

- **Cedar Breaks National Monument:** Often overshadowed by its more famous cousins, Cedar Breaks is likened to a miniature Bryce Canyon. At over 10,000 feet, the elevation alone is enough to deter large crowds and provide you with a quiet, cooler experience. The amphitheater's sprawling coliseum of rock is a riot of color—a vibrant painting unspoiled by excess spectators. Hiking trails like the Rattlesnake Creek Trail offer solitude and the opportunity to spot wildlife, from porcupines to high-altitude birds.

- **Kodachrome Basin State Park:** With a name inspired by a popular type of color film, Kodachrome Basin lives up to its moniker with 64 monolithic stone spires dusted in hues of red, orange, and white. It's a photographer's paradise that remains pleasantly under-visited. Trails like Angel's Palace Trail offer a short hike with rewarding views and quiet contemplation spots. For those willing to explore deeper, the park's backcountry routes promise solitude with a backdrop of stunning rock formations.

- **Goblin Valley State Park:** Imagine a playground designed by nature herself, specifically for the fanciful or the introspective. Goblin Valley, with its bizarre and bewitching hoodoos—mushroom-shaped rock pinnacles—feels otherworldly and is far from the usual tourist itinerary. You can wander among these "goblins" in relative solitude, especially if you visit during off-peak months or at sunrise when even the early birds are few.

- **Grand Staircase-Escalante National Monument:** This is a place of vast and varied landscapes, where every turn brings something awe-inspiring and new. It's a monumental expanse of canyons, arches, and cliffs that remain one of the last explored areas in the Lower 48. For those who truly want to disconnect and disappear into nature, the backroads and trails of Grand Staircase-Escalante offer the perfect escape. From slot canyons like Peek-a-Boo and Spooky Gulch to more secluded areas like Coyote Gulch, the monument invites solitude-seeking adventurers with open arms.

- **Capitol Reef National Park's Backcountry:** While the front country of Capitol Reef can occasionally gather crowds, the park's vast backcountry is a quiet haven for those who trek further. Routes like the Cathedral Valley loop, with its massive monoliths and panoramic vistas, provide a sense of seclusion and perspective that is often lost in more frequented spots. Here, you can drive or hike for miles without seeing another soul, surrounded by the raw beauty of the unspoiled high desert.

- **Buckskin Gulch:** Buckskin Gulch claims the title of the longest and deepest slot canyon in the Southwest, offering an immersive experience that feels like stepping into the narrow creases of the earth. The trek through this slot canyon is not for the faint of heart, requiring preparation and sometimes a permit, but the reward is unparalleled privacy and the kind of quiet that amplifies every footstep and whisper of wind.

Comparative Analysis of Popular vs. Less Crowded Locations

In the majestic realm of Southern Utah, where the landscapes seem painted by the divine hand of nature itself, the traveler is often faced with a choice: follow the crowds to the well-known icons or stray off the beaten path to discover solitude in less-trodden locales. This chapter dives into how to choose alternatives to popular spots without compromising on the breathtaking experiences Southern Utah is famed for.

The Allure of the Popular

Southern Utah's popular destinations—Zion National Park's Angel's Landing, Arches National Park's Delicate Arch, and Bryce Canyon's Amphitheater—draw crowds for good reason. These landmarks offer stunning, accessible vistas that encapsulate the profound beauty of the area. For many, these sites are bucket list destinations, featured prominently in travel brochures and Instagram feeds across the globe.

However, with fame comes the inevitable crowds. During peak seasons, these spots can feel more like a bustling city park than a serene wilderness, which might dilute the very experience of awe and wonder that drew visitors in the first place.

Finding the Road Less Traveled

Choosing less crowded locations doesn't mean sacrificing the quality of your adventure; it simply means adjusting your lens to appreciate a different kind of beauty. Here's how to find and enjoy these hidden alternatives:

Alternate Sites Within Popular Parks

Each popular national park houses lesser-known gems that can offer similar awe without the crowds. For example:

- **Instead of Angel's Landing in Zion,** consider hiking the Kolob Terrace section. Here, the Middle Fork of Taylor Creek trail presents a tranquil alternative, featuring a quiet walk to double arch alcoves and old homesteads without the congestion.

- **Instead of Delicate Arch in Arches,** head to the lesser-visited Broken Arch or Sand Dune Arch. These features offer stunning formations with a fraction of the foot traffic.

- **Instead of Bryce Canyon's Amphitheater,** explore the park's Fairyland Loop. This longer, more challenging trail offers equally stunning views and more chances for quiet contemplation.

- **State Parks as Stand-ins for National Parks**

Utah's state parks are significantly less trafficked but are no less spectacular than their national counterparts. Consider these swaps:

- **Instead of Arches National Park,** visit Dead Horse Point State Park. The vistas here rival those of the Grand

Canyon, with panoramic overlooks of the Colorado River and Canyonlands.

- **Instead of Zion National Park,** explore Snow Canyon State Park. With its petrified dunes and lava tubes, Snow Canyon offers a diverse landscape that's perfect for those looking to avoid the Zion crowds.

Timing Your Visits

Sometimes, the difference between a crowded experience and a solitary one is simply a matter of timing. Visiting popular spots at sunrise or during the off-season can dramatically decrease the number of encounters with other tourists. For example, visiting Bryce Canyon's popular Sunrise Point at actual sunrise offers phenomenal lighting for photographs and ensures fewer people.

Comparative Advantages: Popular vs. Less Crowded

Pros of Popular Locations:

- **Accessibility:** More popular spots often have better facilities and are more accessible to visitors with mobility issues.

- **Iconic Views:** There's a reason these places are on postcards. The views are often uniquely spectacular, offering the quintessential Southern Utah experience.

Pros of Less Crowded Locations:

- **Tranquility:** Less foot traffic means more opportunities to connect with nature without interruption.

- **Wildlife Opportunities:** Animals are more likely to appear in areas that aren't crowded with humans.

- **Personal Satisfaction:** There's something profoundly rewarding about discovering a place that feels untouched and personal.

Integrating the Best of Both Worlds

For the ultimate Southern Utah experience, a balanced itinerary that includes both popular and lesser-known destinations is ideal. This approach allows you to soak in the famous landmarks while also embracing the solitude and unique beauty of the region's hidden corners.

Start your trip with a visit to a popular spot at a strategic time—perhaps a sunrise hike. Then, as the crowds begin to swell, they retreat to the lesser-known areas. This strategy allows you to experience the highlights without the downside of heavy traffic and contributes to a richer, more varied experience of what Southern Utah offers.

By carefully choosing where and when to visit, you can craft an itinerary that offers the best of both worlds—iconic landscapes and serene solitude.

Capitol Reef National Park

Nestled in the heart of Utah's red rock country, Capitol Reef National Park is a hidden gem among the more widely visited giants of the Southwest. It stands as a tribute to the raw, undiluted beauty of nature, often overlooked yet brimming with geological marvels and historical tales. This park offers a more subdued, intimate experience with the wilderness, characterized by its unique geological features, rich cultural heritage, and the serene solitude available during its off-peak seasons.

Geological Features

Capitol Reef National Park is a geological masterpiece, marked prominently by the Waterpocket Fold, a striking 100-mile-long wrinkle on the earth's surface known as a monocline. This dramatic earth fold has created a backbone-like structure that dominates the landscape, with layers of colorful sandstone, shale, and limestone that tell tales of ancient environments, from deserts to shallow seas.

The park's geology is not just diverse but also vibrant, displaying a palette of colors that change with the sunlight. Among its standout features are the Cathedral Valley, a less-traveled area of the park with monolithic sandstone formations resembling cathedrals, and the Hickman Bridge, a natural arch formed through the erosion of rock. It offers a splendid hike and photographic opportunities beneath its span.

Other significant formations include the Capitol Domes, aptly named for resembling capitol building domes due to their whitish Navajo Sandstone with rounded tops, and the Chimney Rock. This towering spire stands sentinel at the park's western entrance. These formations, along with deeply carved canyons and sprawling mesas, provide a rugged terrain that appeals to geologists and adventurers alike.

Historical Significance

Capitol Reef National Park is drenched in human history that dates back over 10,000 years. The area was first inhabited by Native American cultures, including the Fremont people, who left behind petroglyphs etched into rock faces, showcasing men, animals, and mysterious symbols whose meanings are still debated by historians today.

In the more recent past, Mormon pioneers settled in the area in the 1880s, establishing the community of Fruita. The park still houses remnants of this settlement, including orchards where visitors can pick fresh fruit, historic barns, and the one-room

Fruita Schoolhouse, painting a vivid picture of early settler life. The Fruita Rural Historic District offers a tangible connection to the past, reflecting the hardy spirit and ingenuity of those who cultivated this stark, challenging landscape.

The park's history is not just about human endeavor but also about conservation. It was designated a national monument in 1937 and elevated to a national park in 1971, ensuring the preservation of its vast ecological and historical treasures for future generations.

Off-Peak Seasons

While Capitol Reef National Park is enchanting year-round, visiting during the off-peak seasons—late fall, winter, and early spring—offers a unique opportunity to enjoy the park with fewer distractions and lower visitor numbers. Late fall brings cooler temperatures and a display of autumnal colors in the lower parts of the park, making it ideal for those who wish to enjoy the natural scenery in solitude.

Winter transforms the park into a quiet, snowy wonderland rarely seen by tourists. The snow-capped rock formations provide a stark contrast to the usual reds and oranges, offering a new perspective and photographic opportunities. Although some roads and trails may be inaccessible due to snow, the main roads are generally plowed, allowing visitors to explore the park's central areas.

Early spring is another favorable time to visit, as the snow melts, filling the creeks and revealing lush greenery and wildflowers that starkly contrast the red rock. Visitor numbers are still low, and the weather is generally mild, making it ideal for hiking and camping.

Each off-peak season in Capitol Reef offers a different palette and mood, providing solitude and a deeper connection with nature that can be hard to achieve during the busier months. Whether it's the golden glow of late fall, the serene silence of winter, or the rejuvenating burst of spring, Capitol Reef's off-peak seasons are a treasure chest for crowd haters and nature lovers alike.

Weekday vs. Weekend Visits

For those seeking the solitude that Capitol Reef National Park can offer, visiting on a weekday rather than a weekend can markedly enhance the experience. The contrast between weekday and weekend traffic is palpable, with weekdays offering a near-private viewing of the park's grandeur.

Benefits of Weekday Visits:

- **Reduced Crowds:** The most immediate benefit of a weekday visit is the significant reduction in the number of visitors. This means less noise and interruptions and more access to popular sites without the wait.

- **Enhanced Wildlife Viewing:** With fewer people around, wildlife is likelier to appear along trails and in natural habitats. This can be the perfect opportunity for avid nature watchers to observe the park's diverse fauna in a more natural setting.

- **Better Photographic Opportunities:** Photography enthusiasts will find weekdays ideal for capturing the park's unobstructed natural beauty. With fewer tourists photobombing the landscapes, one can take the time to set up the perfect shot.

- **More Personal Interaction:** On quieter weekdays, park staff are more available to answer questions and engage in more in-depth discussions about the park, providing a richer educational experience.

Time of Day Strategies

Choosing the right time of day to visit popular trails in Capitol Reef can greatly affect your experience. Early mornings and late afternoons offer unique advantages for avid hikers and photographers.

Early Morning Visits:

- **Serene Start:** There's a special kind of peace that comes with being one of the first on the trail. The early morning light is magical for photos, and the cooler temperatures make for a more comfortable hike.

- **Wildlife Activity:** Many animals are more active in the cooler hours of the morning, so early risers are likely to spot more wildlife.

- **Beat the Heat:** Especially during the hotter months, hiking in the early morning can be far more pleasant. This allows you to finish your adventure before the midday sun intensifies.

Late Afternoon Visits:

- **Golden Hour Glow:** For photographers, the late afternoon light, known as the golden hour, creates dramatic shadows and beautifully highlights the red rock formations.

- **Evening Cool Down:** As the temperature begins to drop, late afternoon hikes become more enjoyable, and the setting sun offers a cooling respite.

- **Night Sky Viewing:** Staying into the evening provides an opportunity to witness one of the park's spectacular night skies, with stargazing conditions among the best in the world.

Exploring Lesser-Known Areas

Capitol Reef's vastness means that beyond the popular trails, numerous lesser-known areas offer tranquil escapes and unique sights without the crowds.

Cathedral Valley:

- **Remote and Majestic:** Accessible by a rugged loop road that requires a high-clearance vehicle, Cathedral Valley is home to monolithic sandstone formations that tower over the valley floor. The solitude in this part of the park is profound.

- **Iconic Formations:** Temples of the Sun and Moon in Cathedral Valley are particularly striking at sunrise and sunset, where the play of light and shadow brings the landscape to life.

The Waterpocket Fold:

- **Geological Marvel:** The Fold stretches nearly 100 miles and forms the park's spine. It's less trafficked than the

Fruita area and offers a backcountry experience full of rugged trails and expansive views.

- **Backcountry Trails:** Trails like the Strike Valley Overlook and Burro Wash provide immersive experiences into the heart of the Waterpocket Fold's stark, rugged terrain.

Exploring these areas promises a deeper sense of discovery and a personal connection with the park's quieter, undisturbed sides.

Sample Itineraries for Crowded Days

Even on the busiest days at Capitol Reef National Park, a well-structured itinerary can help you avoid the crowds and find your peaceful corner of the park. Here's how to navigate the park strategically:

Morning: Gifford House and Fruita Area

- **Start Early:** Beat the crowds and the heat by starting your day early with a visit to the Gifford House. Grab a freshly baked pie or some homemade preserves— delicious souvenirs from your trip.

- **Quick Stops at Popular Sites:** Early mornings are also ideal for visiting popular spots like the Petroglyph Panel, which is just a few minutes' drive from Fruita. This allows you to enjoy these sights with minimal interruption before the bulk of the day's visitors arrive.

Midday: Scenic Drive and Picnic

- **Drive the Capitol Reef Scenic Drive:** As the park starts to fill up, take a leisurely drive along the Scenic Drive. This route takes you deep into the park's heart with less foot traffic and stunning views from the comfort of your car.

- **Picnic Lunch:** Stop at one of the less frequented pullouts for a picnic lunch. The Grand Wash or Capitol Gorge, accessed from the Scenic Drive, offers shaded spots ideal for a midday break.

Afternoon: Sulphur Creek

- **Hike Sulphur Creek:** This lesser-known hike can be a perfect afternoon adventure. The hike involves some water wading, which makes it less appealing to casual tourists and offers a cooler option during the hotter parts of the day.

Evening: Sunset and Stargazing

- **Sunset at Panorama Point:** End your day with a sunset view at Panorama Point, a less crowded alternative to the more popular Sunset Point.

- **Stargazing:** Capitol Reef is a certified International Dark Sky Park. After sunset, stay a while longer to enjoy some of the best stargazing in the world, away from the day crowds.

Flexible Itinerary Ideas

Capitol Reef's varied landscapes and attractions offer ample opportunities for spontaneous exploration, depending on the day's crowd levels. Here are some flexible itinerary ideas:

High Crowd Levels:

- **Explore the Orchards:** When the main trails and visitor centers are crowded, the park's historic orchards provide a serene alternative for fruit picking in solitude.

- **Visit the Goosenecks Overlook and Sunset Point:** These spots are typically less crowded and offer spectacular views, perfect for impromptu visits when other areas feel too congested.

Moderate Crowd Levels:

- **Capitol Gorge Trail:** On days when crowd levels are manageable, this trail offers a good mix of interesting rock formations and historic inscriptions with enough space to avoid feeling overcrowded.

- **Hickman Bridge during Off-Peak Hours:** Plan to visit this popular spot early in the morning or later in the afternoon when most visitors are elsewhere.

Low Crowd Levels:

- **Strike Valley Overlook:** Access this remote part of the Waterpocket Fold for breathtaking views of the park's backbone. The drive and subsequent hike are best enjoyed when the park is at its quietest.

- **Hall's Creek Narrows:** For a full-day adventure, head to this remote area where you're unlikely to encounter many other visitors.

Off-the-Beaten-Path Hikes

For those seeking solitude and unique natural beauty, Capitol Reef has several less frequented off-the-beaten-path hikes that offer stunning vistas and intimate encounters with the park's wilder side.

Cassidy Arch Trail:

Despite its beauty, Cassidy Arch Trail sees fewer visitors than other park areas, possibly due to its moderate difficulty. The trail leads to a breathtaking natural arch that rivals some of the state's more famous arches.

Navajo Knobs:

This strenuous hike is for those looking to get away from the main tourist areas and enjoy a challenging trek. The panoramic views from the top are some of the best in the park, offering a 360-degree vista of the entire region.

The Golden Throne Trail:

Less known than other trails, Golden Throne offers a peaceful hike with spectacular views of the Capitol Dome and its surroundings. The trail isn't particularly long, but it ascends steadily, offering a good workout and rewarding views.

Each of these trails provides a different perspective of Capitol Reef's lesser-known landscapes, ideal for those looking to explore beyond the standard tourist paths. Whether you're navigating a crowded day or looking for a spontaneous adventure, these itineraries and hikes offer numerous ways to experience the park's profound beauty without the hustle and bustle.

Wildlife Viewing and Nature Photography

Observing wildlife in Capitol Reef National Park offers a thrilling connection to nature, but it requires respect and responsibility. The key to successful wildlife viewing and photography is to maintain a balance between observation and conservation, ensuring minimal disturbance to the natural habits and habitats of the creatures you're observing.

Best Practices for Observing Wildlife:

- **Keep a Safe Distance:** Always maintain a safe distance from wildlife. Use binoculars or a long lens for close-up views and photos. This protects you and the animals and preserves their natural behaviors.

- **Stay Quiet and Patient:** Wildlife is more likely to appear if you are quiet and minimize movements. Patience is essential; often, the best sightings come to those who wait silently.

- **Use the Right Equipment:** Wildlife photographers must have a good-quality zoom lens. This allows them to capture detailed images without needing to get too close.

- **Follow Park Regulations:** Heed all park rules regarding wildlife interaction. Feeding, touching, or disturbing wildlife is prohibited as it can alter their natural behaviors and endanger both the animals and park visitors.

- **Respect Their Space:** Be particularly cautious during sensitive times such as mating, nesting, or raising young. Disturbances can have serious repercussions on wildlife populations.

Stargazing Opportunities

Capitol Reef National Park is renowned for its dark skies, making it a prime location for stargazing. The absence of light pollution ensures that visitors can enjoy an unobstructed view of the cosmos.

<u>Tips for Enjoying the Night Sky:</u>

- **Check the Moon Calendar:** The moon's phase can greatly affect your stargazing experience. A new moon is ideal for viewing stars, as the sky is darkest then.

- **Use Red Flashlights:** Red lights minimize light pollution and will not disrupt your night vision as white lights do.

- **Find a Remote Spot:** Although the whole park benefits from dark skies, the further you are from any source of light, the better your viewing will be. Areas like Cathedral Valley are particularly good for their remoteness and unobstructed horizons.

- **Allow Time for Your Eyes to Adjust:** Spend at least 30 minutes in the dark to let your eyes adjust fully to low-light conditions. This will significantly improve your vision.

- **Join a Ranger Program:** If available, attend a ranger-led night sky program to gain deeper insights and learn about the celestial features you're observing.

Where to Stay

Choosing where to stay when visiting Capitol Reef National Park can greatly affect your experience, especially if you're looking to avoid crowds. Staying outside the park in nearby towns supports local communities and provides a quieter, more relaxed environment.

Options for Lodging Outside the Park:

- **Torrey:** Just eight miles west of the park, Torrey is a small town with a range of accommodations, from motels and bed and breakfasts to inns. The town is small enough to offer a quiet stay but sufficiently equipped with necessary amenities and restaurants.

- **Bicknell:** Located about 20 minutes from the park, Bicknell is even smaller than Torrey but offers a quaint, peaceful base for exploring the area.

- **Loa:** For those looking for a truly local experience, Loa is a great option. About a 25-minute drive from the park, it provides basic services and a handful of lodging options.

- **Camping:** For those who prefer to stay closer to nature, several campgrounds and RV parks are available in and around these towns. These offer a more rustic stay with spectacular night sky views.

Dining Recommendations

While Capitol Reef National Park itself isn't known for a bustling culinary scene, the surrounding towns, particularly Torrey, offer charming and less touristy dining options that provide a taste of local flavors along with international cuisine. Venturing into these small towns supports local businesses and provides a more authentic and intimate dining experience. Here are some recommended eateries where you can enjoy good food and a break from the more crowded tourist spots:

Cafe Diablo in Torrey

- **Cuisine:** Southwestern with a gourmet twist.

- **Highlight:** Cafe Diablo offers a creative menu that includes dishes such as rattlesnake cakes and Utah trout. The restaurant's eclectic decor and presentation make it a memorable place to dine.

- **Why It's Less Touristy:** Although popular among those who know the area, its unique menu items tend to attract a more adventurous eater, keeping the mainstream crowds at bay.

Slackers Burger Joint in Torrey

- **Cuisine:** American Diner.

- **Highlight:** Known for its burgers and shakes, Slackers is a no-frills diner with a friendly atmosphere and hearty, comforting food.

- **Why It's Less Touristy:** Its simple, unpretentious menu and casual setting make it more popular with locals than tourists, offering visitors a genuine small-town American diner experience.

The Rim Rock Restaurant

- **Cuisine:** Traditional American with options for fine dining.

- **Highlight:** Situated a bit off the main road, The Rim Rock Restaurant offers stunning views of the surrounding cliffs. The menu includes steak, seafood, and vegetarian options, catering to a variety of tastes.

- **Why It's Less Touristy:** Its location and slightly higher-end menu appeal more to those seeking a quiet dinner with a view, away from the tourist crowds.

Capitol Reef Inn & Cafe

- **Cuisine:** American and Mexican.

- **Highlight:** A cozy spot that serves up a mix of American classics and Mexican dishes. The cafe is part of the Capitol Reef Inn, giving it a homey feel.

- **Why It's Less Touristy:** Being part of a small inn, the cafe tends to draw more inn guests than outside tourists, providing a quieter, more relaxed meal.

The Gifford Homestead

- **Cuisine:** Bakery and Snack shop.

- **Highlight:** Located inside Capitol Reef National Park, this historic site offers freshly baked pies, cinnamon rolls, and loaves of bread, along with local preserves and ice cream.

- **Why It's Less Touristy:** While it is inside the park, The Gifford Homestead offers a more historical and local eating experience that provides a moment's rest from typical park dining options.

Exploring these local eateries allows you to enjoy a slice of rural Utah's hospitality and culinary creativity, enhancing your visit to Capitol Reef with flavors as rich and memorable as the landscapes.

Grand Staircase-Escalante National Monument

Grand Staircase-Escalante National Monument, sprawling across southern Utah's high desert plateau, offers a breathtaking expanse of wilderness that seems to stretch the very fabric of time. It's a place where solitude is not merely a concept but a palpable entity, winding through the sinuous canyons and towering above the endless vistas. This vast, less trodden landscape serves as an introvert's paradise, where one can wander for hours, or even days, without crossing paths with another soul—unless, of course, you count the occasional desert tortoise or peregrine falcon.

Geological Features

The geological features of Grand Staircase-Escalante are nothing short of a geological symphony, played out over millions of years and written in the layers of sandstone, limestone, and shale. The monument's name itself—an evocative nod to the series of huge, descending terraces that dominate the landscape—captures the imagination and beckons explorers to its many secluded corners.

At the heart of this grand geological exhibit is the Escalante River Canyon, a marvel of erosive force. Here, the river has carved intricate patterns into the rock, creating a labyrinth of narrow slot canyons that twist and turn in shadowy splendor. The Peek-a-Boo and Spooky Gulch slot canyons are particularly compelling; their walls are so close at points that one can touch both sides at once, yet so artfully carved that each step forward feels like moving through a sculpture gallery designed by nature itself.

The monument's upper section, the Grand Staircase, descends from Bryce Canyon towards the Paria River in a sequence of cliffs and terraces, each layer a different hue—pink cliffs, grey cliffs, white cliffs, vermilion cliffs, and chocolate cliffs. This staircase is a veritable timeline of Earth's middle Cretaceous period, with each step down a journey further back in time.

In the lower sections, the vast Kaiparowits Plateau offers a starkly beautiful, rugged terrain punctuated by expansive views and monumental silence. The plateau's isolation and difficult access contribute to its untouched feel, making it a haven for those seeking both solitude and wilderness.

Historical Significance

The monument's history is as layered as its terrain. Long before it became a national monument in 1996, Grand Staircase-Escalante was home to ancient Native American tribes, including the Ancestral Puebloans and the Fremont people, whose rock art and granaries are etched into the canyon walls. These sites tell silent tales of adaptation, survival, and artistry in an unforgiving landscape.

In the 19th century, Mormon pioneers found their way into these parts, carving out a harsh, isolated existence among the canyons and mesas. The town of Escalante, one of the last populated places to be mapped in the continental United States, was settled by these pioneers, whose descendants still call the area home, adding a living human layer to the region's historical jumble.

The monument itself was a latecomer to the national scene, established by President Bill Clinton under the Antiquities Act. Its designation was not without controversy, reflecting a modern chapter in the ongoing American discussion about land use and conservation. Today, Grand Staircase-Escalante serves as a crucial research area for paleontologists and geologists, with numerous dinosaur fossils and geological formations offering clues to Earth's evolutionary saga.

Off-Peak Seasons

For the introverted traveler, the off-peak seasons in Grand Staircase-Escalante promise vast stretches of solitude without interrupting crowds. Late fall, winter, and early spring offer the ideal times to explore this rugged wilderness with minimal human contact.

- **Late Fall:** The air is crisp, the summer heat a fading memory, and the tourist traffic has dwindled. The lower angles of the sun cast long shadows that enhance the textures of the rock formations, making it a fantastic season for photography.

- **Winter:** Snow rarely finds its way into these dry climates, but when it does, it transforms the landscape into a quiet, monochrome wonderland. Few travelers venture here during the colder months, leaving the canyons and mesas in profound silence.

- **Early Spring:** As the winter chill wanes, the wildflowers begin their tentative bloom, dusting the desert with color. The streams and waterfalls, fed by melting snows from the higher elevations, add a melodious backdrop to hikes through the canyons.

Visiting during these quieter months enhances the feeling of isolation and connection with nature and also provides a unique perspective on the monument's timeless beauty.

Weekday vs. Weekend Visits

For those who find sanctuary in solitude, visiting Grand Staircase-Escalante National Monument during the weekdays is akin to finding an unexplored treasure trove. The differences between weekday and weekend visitations are palpable and can significantly alter the nature of your experience in this expansive wilderness.

Benefits of Weekday Visits:

- **Reduced Crowds:** Naturally, weekdays see fewer visitors. This decrease in foot traffic allows for a more personal connection with nature, where the only interruption might be the rustle of wildlife or the whisper of the wind.

- **Unhurried Exploration:** With fewer people around, you can take your time exploring trails and sites without feeling rushed or crowded. This is particularly beneficial in areas where narrow canyons or delicate ecosystems make space a precious commodity.

- **Greater Wildlife Activity:** Animals are more active when human presence is minimized. Weekdays provide a better opportunity for wildlife viewing, as the animals are less disturbed by human activity.

- **Enhanced Photographic Opportunities:** Fewer people mean fewer obstructions for photographers. You can take your time setting up shots without worrying about someone walking into the frame or waiting for a clear moment.

Visiting during the week gives the feeling of having the monument mostly to yourself, enhancing the feeling of escapism that many seek in such natural settings.

Time of Day Strategies

Timing is crucial when planning your visit to Grand Staircase-Escalante, especially if you aim to maximize your experience on the trails and at popular sites. The stark differences in landscape visibility and temperatures between early morning and late afternoon can dramatically affect your excursion.

Early Morning Visits:

- **Advantages:** Early morning is ideal for beating both the heat and the crowds. The soft morning light enhances the natural colors of the rock formations, making it a perfect time for photography. Additionally, temperatures are cooler, making hikes more comfortable.

- **Experience:** Start your day with a sunrise view at one of the monument's high vantage points, such as Sunrise Point near Escalante. The quiet of the morning, combined with the breathtaking colors of dawn, provides a peaceful and invigorating start to the day.

Late Afternoon Visits:

- **Advantages:** The late afternoon light, known as the golden hour, casts a warm glow over the landscape, creating ideal lighting conditions for photography.

Temperatures begin to cool, making it a pleasant time for hiking.

- **Experience:** Trails like the Lower Calf Creek Falls become magical in the late afternoon as the sun's rays illuminate the waterfalls and high canyon walls. Ending your day with a sunset in this setting can be a tranquil and reflective experience.

Exploring Lesser-Known Areas

While Grand Staircase-Escalante is renowned for its vastness and beauty, many of its lesser-known areas still need to be explored. These areas offer solitude and unique natural features without the crowds.

Cathedral Valley:

- **Features:** Known for its towering sandstone monoliths and stark desert beauty, Cathedral Valley is accessible via a rugged loop road that requires high-clearance, four-wheel-drive vehicles. The area offers spectacular views of the Temples of the Sun and Moon, massive stone structures that rise dramatically from the valley floor.

- **Experience:** Exploring Cathedral Valley feels like stepping onto another planet. Its remote nature discourages large crowds, making it a perfect spot for those seeking isolation and spectacular geological formations.

The Waterpocket Fold:

- **Features:** This 100-mile-long buckle in the Earth's surface offers various hiking opportunities, from slot canyons to elevated vistas. The Fold's remote location and challenging access points ensure that it remains one of the less crowded areas of the monument.

- **Experience:** Hiking in the Waterpocket Fold can be as rewarding as it is challenging. Routes like the Strike Valley Overlook trail offer secluded paths and breathtaking views of the Capitol Reef's backcountry, providing a deep sense of immersion in the natural world.

By venturing into these less-visited areas, you escape the crowds and discover some of Grand Staircase-Escalante's most awe-inspiring landscapes, which remain as untouched and majestic as they have for centuries.

Sample Itineraries for Crowded Days

Navigating Grand Staircase-Escalante National Monument on crowded days requires strategic planning to avoid the most popular areas while still experiencing the park's stunning beauty.

Here's how to structure your visit to make the most out of a busy day:

Morning: Early Start at Devil's Garden

- **Plan:** Begin your day at Devil's Garden, arriving just after sunrise. This area is less crowded in the early hours, allowing you to explore the whimsical rock formations and arches in relative solitude.

- **Activity:** Take a quick, scenic hike around the area, capturing photos of the natural arches and hoodoos illuminated by the soft morning light.

Mid-Morning: Drive Along Hole-in-the-Rock Road

- **Plan:** As the crowds start to gather, take a scenic drive along Hole-in-the-Rock Road. This less frequented road offers numerous pullouts with fantastic views and short trails that are usually quiet.

- **Activity:** Stop at Zebra Slot Canyon for a brief hike. Arriving before late morning will help you avoid the groups that often form later in the day.

Afternoon: Escalante River Trail

- **Plan:** In the afternoon, head to the Escalante River Trail. This trail is longer and tends to be less crowded, especially further along the path.

- **Activity:** Enjoy a leisurely hike along the river, taking in the serene environment and natural beauty without the rush of more crowded sites.

Late Afternoon: Sunset at Sunset Arch

- **Plan:** Conclude your day with a drive to Sunset Arch, arriving an hour before sunset. This lesser-known gem provides a peaceful setting to watch the sunset and is typically quiet in the evenings.

- **Activity:** Set up a picnic and relax as you watch the sky and landscape change colors at sunset.

Flexible Itinerary Ideas

Exploring Grand Staircase-Escalante can be a dynamic adventure; adjusting your plans based on crowd levels ensures a more enjoyable experience:

High Crowd Levels:

- **Morning:** Start with less accessible areas like the backroads of Cottonwood Canyon Road, where fewer tourists venture.

- **Afternoon:** When outdoor sites become too crowded, explore local museums or visitor centers, such as the Escalante Heritage Center.

Moderate Crowd Levels:

- **Morning:** Visit moderately popular sites like the Lower Calf Creek Falls early in the day before crowds peak.

- **Afternoon:** Head to nearby towns like Boulder for local eats and some quaint shopping, offering a break from the park's busier areas.

Low Crowd Levels:

- **Be Spontaneous:** With fewer visitors, take the opportunity to explore popular spots that are usually crowded or attempt longer trails like Death Hollow.

Off-the-Beaten-Path Hikes

For those seeking solitude and natural beauty away from the usual paths, Grand Staircase-Escalante offers several stunning, less frequented hikes:

Cassidy Arch Trail:

- **Features:** Although located in the nearby Capitol Reef National Park, Cassidy Arch Trail is a fantastic option for those exploring the broader region. The trail is moderately challenging and leads to a breathtaking natural arch that offers spectacular photo opportunities and fewer crowds.

- **Experience:** Enjoy the thrill of hiking to an arch that rivals the more famous ones in Arches National Park, with a fraction of the visitors.

Dry Fork Narrows, Peek-a-Boo and Spooky Gulch Slot Canyons:

- **Features:** These slot canyons offer an adventurous hike that is slightly off the typical tourist radar due to the difficulty of some passages.

- **Experience:** Clamber through narrow, winding canyons where the walls are so close you can touch both sides simultaneously. The eerie silence and stunning rock formations make this hike unforgettable.

Coyote Gulch:

- **Features:** A longer and more challenging trek, Coyote Gulch is ideal for those wanting a full-day hike or an overnight adventure.

- **Experience:** Hike along a flowing stream that leads to towering cliffs, natural arches, and ancient Native American rock art.

These trails are perfect for those who wish to explore deeper into the wilderness and experience the untamed beauty of Grand Staircase-Escalante without the crowds. Each offers a unique journey into the heart of Utah's spectacular high desert landscape.

Wildlife Viewing and Nature Photography

Grand Staircase-Escalante National Monument offers abundant opportunities for wildlife viewing and nature photography, but it requires a respectful and thoughtful approach to minimize disturbance to the natural habitat.

Best Practices for Observing Wildlife:

- **Keep Your Distance:** Always maintain a safe and respectful distance from wildlife. Use binoculars or a telephoto lens to observe or photograph animals without getting too close. This helps prevent stress on the animals and keeps you safe.

- **Stay Quiet:** Move quietly and speak softly when near wildlife. Loud noises can startle animals, causing stress and potentially forcing them to flee, which can deplete their energy reserves.

- **Minimize Movement:** Sudden movements can also disturb animals. If you're watching or photographing wildlife, try to remain still and make slow, deliberate movements.

- **Respect Their Space:** Avoid approaching nests, dens, or any area that wildlife has chosen for resting or feeding. Disturbing these spaces can have detrimental effects on animal behavior and survival.

- **No Feeding:** Feeding wildlife alters their natural behaviors and diet and can lead to health problems or dangerous dependencies on human-provided food.

- **Educate Yourself:** Knowing the behavior and needs of wildlife in Grand Staircase-Escalante can enhance your experience and reduce the likelihood of causing distress to the animals.

By following these guidelines, visitors can enjoy watching wildlife while ensuring they have no negative impact on the natural environment.

Stargazing Opportunities

Grand Staircase-Escalante, with its remote location and minimal light pollution, is an ideal spot for stargazing. Here's how to maximize your experience under the stars.

Tips for Enjoying the Night Sky:

- **Check the Lunar Calendar:** Plan your stargazing around the new moon when the sky is darkest. Avoid full moon nights, as the moonlight can obscure dimmer stars.

- **Find an Open Area:** Wide-open spaces away from cliffs and tall structures will give you a broader view of the sky. The desert landscapes within the monument offer unobstructed views of the heavens.

- **Let Your Eyes Adjust:** Allow your eyes about 30 minutes to adapt to the darkness. Avoid looking at bright lights during this time, as they can disrupt night vision. Use a red flashlight to navigate, as red light has less impact on night vision.

- **Use Minimal Equipment:** A simple pair of binoculars or a basic telescope can enhance your viewing experience, but much of the Milky Way and many constellations can be seen with the naked eye.

- **Stargazing Apps:** Use apps to help identify stars, planets, and constellations. Ensure your phone's screen is set to a red night mode to minimize light pollution.

By embracing these practices, you can enjoy a spectacular view of the cosmos that few places on Earth can match.

Where to Stay

To fully experience Grand Staircase-Escalante without the crowds, consider staying in nearby towns which offer various accommodations ranging from rustic to refined.

Torrey:

- **Characteristics:** Just west of Capitol Reef National Park and about an hour's drive to the monument, Torrey offers a range of lodging options from motels and inns to bed and breakfasts.

- **Recommended Stay:** The Rim Rock Inn offers views of the red rock cliffs and has a restaurant on-site, making it a convenient and scenic option.

Boulder:

- **Characteristics:** Located to the north of the monument, Boulder provides a quieter, more secluded base for exploring the area.

- **Recommended Stay:** Boulder Mountain Lodge is known for its hospitality and access to stunning natural surroundings.

Escalante:

- **Characteristics:** This small town is directly adjacent to the monument and is a gateway to its many trails and attractions.

- **Recommended Stay:** The Slot Canyons Inn Bed & Breakfast offers comfortable accommodations and is ideally situated for exploring the canyons.

Staying in these towns helps you avoid the crowds and supports local economies, offering a deeper connection to the region through its communities.

Dining Recommendations

Exploring the culinary offerings in and around Grand Staircase-Escalante National Monument provides a delightful complement to the natural explorations. The area's small towns harbor several local eateries that promise delicious meals without the tourist trappings. Here are some top dining recommendations that let you taste the local flavor while avoiding the typical tourist crowds.

Escalante Outfitters Café (Escalante)

- **Overview:** A favorite among hikers and local adventurers, Escalante Outfitters Café serves hearty, satisfying meals perfect for fueling or recovering from a day in the wilderness. The café is part of a larger outfitting service, which gives it an authentic, local vibe.

- **Specialties:** Don't miss their homemade pizzas and the locally famous chicken pesto sandwich. They also offer excellent breakfast options, with ingredients sourced from local farms whenever possible.

Hell's Backbone Grill & Farm (Boulder)

- **Overview:** Nestled in the small town of Boulder, Hell's Backbone Grill & Farm focuses on sustainable, farm-to-table dining, inspired by the surrounding landscapes and Buddhist principles.

- **Specialties:** Try their blue corn pancakes or the organic lamb and beef meatloaf. The restaurant grows much of its produce on its own farm, ensuring freshness and quality.

Kiva Koffeehouse (Escalante)

- **Overview:** Perched on a cliff with breathtaking views, Kiva Koffeehouse offers a blend of good food and stunning architecture, all crafted from native stone and woods. It's a peaceful spot for a meal, coffee, or dessert.

- **Specialties:** Enjoy a cup of their locally roasted coffee paired with homemade pastries or a light lunch while soaking in the panoramic views.

Burr Trail Grill (Boulder)

- **Overview:** Situated at the junction of Burr Trail and Highway 12, Burr Trail Grill is a casual, laid-back spot known for its friendly service and tasty, uncomplicated food.

- **Specialties:** The burgers are a must-try here, especially the green chili burger. They also serve a variety of sandwiches, salads, and specials like fish tacos.

The Saddlery Cowboy Bar and Steakhouse (Torrey)

- **Overview:** For a taste of local Western culture, The Saddlery Cowboy Bar and Steakhouse in Torrey offers a lively atmosphere and a menu filled with hearty American classics.

- **Specialties:** Steaks are the highlight here, grilled to perfection. On weekends, the place often features live country music and line dancing, adding to the authentic cowboy experience.

These dining spots serve delicious food and provide a genuine local experience, allowing visitors to connect more deeply with the community and culture of Southern Utah.

Each establishment, with its unique charm and specialties, reflects the spirit of the surrounding landscape, making them perfect stops on your journey through Grand Staircase-Escalante.

Cedar Breaks National Monument

Cedar Breaks National Monument, perched high in the Colorado Plateau at over 10,000 feet, is a stunning natural amphitheater stretching three miles across and plunging over 2,000 feet deep. The monument's colossal coliseum of red rock is dramatically marked by some of the clearest skies and air in the country, making it a visual feast but a breath of fresh, crisp air. This high-altitude haven offers a cooler retreat during the blistering summers and a quiet, snow-shrouded sanctuary in the winter.

Geological Features

Cedar Breaks National Monument showcases extraordinary geological formations and processes. The amphitheater, formed by erosion over millions of years, displays a striking array of hoodoos, fins, and spires that paint a vivid picture of nature's artistic prowess. The monument's vibrant colors come from iron oxidizing in the limestone, creating a palette of deep reds, yellows, and purples that are particularly intense at sunrise and sunset.

The area's significant elevation contributes to its unique geological features, including ancient bristlecone pines that skirt the rim of the amphitheater. These gnarled trees, some of the oldest living organisms on Earth, bear witness to the harsh conditions and the slow, persistent sculpting of the landscape by the elements. Cedar Breaks also sits on the edge of the Markagunt Plateau, where volcanic activity millions of years ago laid down layers of ash and lava, contributing to the complex geology of the region.

Throughout the park, trails and viewpoints offer visitors a closer look at the intricate details of the rock formations, from delicate arches to massive stone columns that stand as natural monuments to the power of erosion and time.

Historical Significance

Cedar Breaks National Monument holds deep historical significance, evidenced by its long history of human occupation. Native American tribes, including the Paiute, valued Cedar Breaks as a summer retreat and hunting ground, drawn by its abundant wildlife and medicinal plants. Artifacts and petroglyphs in the area tell stories of these early inhabitants, who navigated the high plateaus and deep canyons of the region for centuries.

In the 19th century, European settlers discovered the area, naming it for the resemblance of its eroded rock formations to city buildings and the juniper trees they mistakenly called cedars. The monument was officially established in 1933, during an era when conservation efforts sought to protect and celebrate the unique landscapes of the American West. Today, Cedar Breaks continues to be a site of scientific study and public awe, offering insight into the natural history and evolving geology of the plateau.

Off-Peak Seasons

Visiting Cedar Breaks during the off-peak seasons can transform the experience into one of solitude and stark beauty. The ideal months for fewer visitors are late fall, winter, and early spring.

- **Late Fall:** As temperatures drop, visitor numbers dwindle, but the monument's beauty remains, highlighted by dustings of early snow against the red rock and remaining golden aspens.

- **Winter:** Access to the amphitheater rim can be limited due to snow, but the park transforms into a winter wonderland, offering snowshoeing and cross-country skiing for the adventurous and hearty. The quiet of a snow-covered Cedar Breaks is profound and picturesque.

- **Early Spring:** Before the summer crowds begin to arrive, early spring can be magical. The snow begins to melt, feeding vibrant new life in the meadows, and the crisp air carries the promise of renewal.

Each of these seasons offers a different perspective of Cedar Breaks, showcasing the monument's year-round appeal and providing a quieter, more reflective visit.

Weekday vs. Weekend Visits

Choosing to visit Cedar Breaks National Monument during weekdays instead of weekends can significantly enhance the tranquility of your experience. The serene, vast landscapes lend themselves perfectly to quiet reflection and leisurely exploration, qualities that are best enjoyed without the hustle and bustle typically found during weekend visits.

Benefits of Weekday Visits:

- **Fewer Crowds:** Naturally, weekdays see a lower volume of visitors. This reduction means more parking and less traffic and more intimate encounters with nature's wonders.

- **Enhanced Wildlife Viewing:** Fewer people mean wildlife is less disturbed, increasing the chances of spotting mule deer, porcupines, or even elusive mountain lions.

- **Personalized Interaction with Park Staff:** Fewer visitors means that park rangers and staff can provide more personalized information, enriching your understanding of the monument's natural and cultural history.

- **Better Photographic Opportunities:** With less crowd interference, photographers can take their time to set up the perfect shot, capturing stunning geological formations and vibrant colors without interruption.

Exploring Cedar Breaks during the weekdays allows for a more thoughtful, immersive experience, perfect for those seeking peace and solitude in nature.

Time of Day Strategies

The time of day you choose to visit Cedar Breaks can drastically affect your experience, especially in terms of lighting and temperature, which are crucial in such a high-elevation environment.

Early Morning Visits:

- **Advantages:** Visiting at sunrise offers spectacular photo opportunities with the amphitheater lit in soft, golden hues and cooler hiking conditions. Morning light provides a unique perspective on the monument's colors and shadows, enhancing the dramatic landscape.

- **Experience:** Trails like the Spectra Point and Ramparts Overlook come alive in the morning light. The early hours also increase the likelihood of wildlife encounters as many animals are active during the cooler parts of the day.

Late Afternoon Visits:

- **Advantages:** As the sun begins to set, the red rocks of Cedar Breaks glow intensely red and orange, offering a different but equally stunning visual experience. Temperatures begin to drop, making hikes more comfortable.

- **Experience:** Viewing the sunset from Point Supreme is particularly breathtaking. The sky often erupts in vibrant colors that reflect off the amphitheater's rocks.

Whether you choose the crisp morning air or the warm afternoon light, both times of day offer unique advantages for experiencing Cedar Breaks National Monument.

Exploring Lesser-Known Areas

While the main amphitheater at Cedar Breaks garners most of the attention, the monument also offers several lesser-known areas that provide tranquility and unique beauty away from the more frequented overlooks and trails.

Rattlesnake Creek Trail:

- **Features:** This less-traveled trail offers a quieter alternative to the more popular hikes. It meanders through ancient forests and meadows, with opportunities to see wildlife and wildflowers, depending on the season.

- **Experience:** The trail is ideal for those seeking solitude and a deeper connection with the natural environment.

It's also excellent for bird watching, as many species are attracted to the less disturbed areas of the park.

Twisted Forest Trail:

- **Features:** A hidden gem, this trail is known for its ancient bristlecone pines, which are among the oldest living organisms on Earth. These gnarled trees tell a story of resilience and beauty, surviving in harsh conditions.

- **Experience:** The trail is short but steep, offering panoramic views and a quiet, reflective hike. It's less known and therefore less frequented, providing a peaceful escape.

Exploring these areas allows for a fuller appreciation of Cedar Breaks' diverse landscape, offering a sense of discovery and isolation that can be rare in more popular national parks.

Sample Itineraries for Crowded Days

Visiting Cedar Breaks National Monument during peak visitor times requires a thoughtful approach to avoid the most crowded areas. Here's an itinerary designed to help you make the most of your visit while steering clear of the busiest spots:

Morning: Early Rise for Alpine Pond Trail

- **Plan:** Start your day early by hitting the Alpine Pond Trail, a less crowded alternative that offers peaceful forest settings and views of the amphitheater from a distance. The morning light and dew bring a fresh and vibrant feel to the trail, enhancing your experience.

- **Activity:** Enjoy a quiet, leisurely hike around the pond, perfect for birdwatching and gentle reflection.

Mid-Morning: Visitor Center and Short Walks

- **Plan:** Visit the Cedar Breaks Visitor Center when it opens. This timing usually beats the rush of visitors who arrive later in the day. Check out the educational exhibits and speak with rangers for insights and updates on less crowded spots.

- **Activity:** Take short walks around the nearby trails or viewpoints that are less likely to accumulate crowds, such as Sunset Trail for a brief and scenic loop.

Afternoon: Drive to North View Overlook

- **Plan:** As the crowds start to peak around the main amphitheater, take a scenic drive to the North View Overlook, a less frequented spot that offers spectacular views of the monument.

- **Activity:** Have a picnic lunch here, enjoying the expansive vistas without the hustle and bustle of the main viewing areas.

Late Afternoon: Spectra Point Overlook

- **Plan:** In the late afternoon, head to Spectra Point Overlook. While this spot can be popular, its visitors often dwindle late in the day.

- **Activity:** The walk to Spectra Point is breathtaking and offers several benches to relax and take in the views as the sun begins to lower, casting beautiful shadows across the amphitheater.

Flexible Itinerary Ideas

The key to enjoying Cedar Breaks National Monument during varying crowd levels is flexibility. Here are some itinerary suggestions that adjust based on the number of visitors:

High Crowd Levels:

- **Morning:** Explore the Rattlesnake Creek Trail, a less-known area where you're less likely to encounter many people.

- **Afternoon:** Visit the local towns around Cedar Breaks, such as Brian Head or Panguitch, where you can enjoy local eateries and small-town charm.

Moderate Crowd Levels:

- **Morning:** Hike the Alpine Pond Trail, which should provide a moderate level of solitude away from the main overlooks.

- **Afternoon:** Check out the Visitor Center and nearby short nature trails, which might have fewer visitors as the day progresses.

Low Crowd Levels:

- **Be spontaneous:** With fewer visitors, explore more popular areas like Point Supreme or Spectra Point, enjoying the main attractions without the usual crowds.

Off-the-Beaten-Path Hikes

For those seeking solitude and unique experiences away from the more traveled paths, Cedar Breaks offers several stunning hikes:

Cassidy Arch Trail:

- **Location:** Located in Capitol Reef National Park, Cassidy Arch Trail offers a wonderful excursion close enough to combine with a trip to Cedar Breaks.

- **Features:** This trail is moderately challenging and culminates at an impressive natural arch that provides spectacular photo opportunities and fewer crowds compared to more popular arches in Utah.

Twisted Forest Trail:

- **Features:** This short but rewarding hike takes you through a forest of ancient bristlecone pines with twisted and gnarled formations that are a photographer's dream.

- **Experience:** Enjoy the quiet and contemplation possible on this less frequented trail, which also offers beautiful views of the Cedar Breaks amphitheater from a unique vantage point.

These off-the-beaten-path hikes enhance your visit with peaceful experiences and immerse you in the stunning natural beauty of the area, far from the typical tourist spots.

Wildlife Viewing and Nature Photography

Cedar Breaks National Monument offers abundant opportunities for wildlife viewing and photography, provided visitors adhere to ethical practices that protect both the wildlife and their habitats.

Best Practices for Wildlife Viewing and Photography:

- **Keep a Respectful Distance:** Always maintain a safe distance from animals to avoid causing them stress or altering their natural behaviors. Use binoculars or a long lens for photography to get a closer look without encroachment.

- **Stay Quiet and Patient:** Animals are more likely to appear and remain in an area if it is quiet. Move slowly and quietly, and use natural cover for observing wildlife to minimize your presence.

- **No Feeding:** Feeding wildlife can harm their health, alter natural behaviors, and increase dependence on human-provided foods. Always observe animals as they are and allow them to forage naturally.

- **Limit Use of Flash:** When photographing wildlife, avoid using flash as it can startle animals, temporarily impair their vision, and disrupt their natural activity patterns.

- **Follow Park Rules:** Heed all park regulations regarding wildlife interaction and photography. These rules are designed to protect both the wildlife and the visitors.

By following these guidelines, visitors can enjoy and capture the beauty of Cedar Breaks' wildlife without causing harm, ensuring that these creatures continue to thrive in their natural environment.

Stargazing Opportunities

Cedar Breaks National Monument is renowned for its pristine dark skies, making it an excellent location for stargazing. Here are some tips to maximize your night-sky viewing experience in this breathtaking setting:

Tips for Stargazing:

- **Check the Moon Phase:** Plan your stargazing around the new moon when the sky is darkest. Avoid times when the moon is full, as its brightness will obscure fainter stars.

- **Use Red Light Flashlights:** To preserve your night vision, use flashlights with red bulbs. Red light has minimal impact on your ability to see the stars.

- **Dress Warmly:** Nights at high elevations can be chilly, even in summer. Bring warm clothing and blankets to stay comfortable while you observe the sky.

- **Allow for Night Vision Adjustment:** Give your eyes at least 15-30 minutes to adjust to the darkness without looking at any bright light sources.

- **Choose a Good Viewing Spot:** The Point Supreme Overlook offers expansive sky views with minimal light pollution. Arrive early to secure a good spot, especially during astronomical events.

These tips will help you enjoy Cedar Breaks' dark skies to their fullest, providing a memorable stargazing experience amidst the quiet and vast wilderness.

Where to Stay

While Cedar Breaks National Monument itself offers limited on-site accommodations, several nearby towns provide a range of lodging options that cater to different preferences and budgets:

Brian Head:

- **Characteristics:** Just a short drive from Cedar Breaks, Brian Head is a mountain town known for its ski resort and offers comfortable accommodations year-round.

- **Options:** Choose from cozy cabins, hotels, and vacation rentals. Cedar Breaks Lodge, offering spa services and dining options, is a popular choice.

Parowan:

- **Characteristics:** Located further from the park, Parowan offers a small-town atmosphere with basic amenities and fewer tourists.

- **Options:** Bed and breakfasts and small motels like the Victorian Rose Country Inn provide a quaint, quiet base for exploring the area.

Panguitch:

- **Characteristics:** This historic town is a bit of a drive from Cedar Breaks but offers a charming and authentic Utah experience.

- **Options:** Panguitch hosts a variety of lodging options, from historic hotels to family-run motels and guesthouses.

Staying in these towns allows easy access to Cedar Breaks, supports local communities, and provides a peaceful retreat after a day of exploring the monument's natural wonders.

Dining Recommendations

Exploring Cedar Breaks National Monument also means discovering the local flavors of the surrounding southern Utah area. While Cedar Breaks itself is remote, the nearby towns offer a variety of dining options that cater to a less touristy crowd, providing authentic and delightful experiences. Here are some choice eateries where you can enjoy the local cuisine away from the typical tourist traps:

The Pizza Cart (Cedar City)

- **Overview:** Located in Cedar City, about a 45-minute drive from Cedar Breaks, The Pizza Cart offers a gourmet, artisan approach to pizza. This local favorite uses fresh, often locally sourced ingredients to create unique wood-fired pizzas.

- **Specialty:** Try their award-winning "Sweet & Spicy" pizza for a blend of unexpected flavors, or the classic "Margherita" for a taste of tradition.

Centro Woodfired Pizzeria (Cedar City)

- **Overview:** Also in Cedar City, Centro Woodfired Pizzeria is renowned for its rustic setting and delicious, freshly made pizzas. The ambiance is cozy, and the woodfired oven is the heart of the restaurant, where each pizza is crafted with care.

- **Specialty:** Their woodfired pizzas are a must-try, especially the "Wild Mushroom" pizza, topped with a variety of mushrooms and truffle oil.

Pastry Pub (Cedar City)

- **Overview:** This casual eatery is perfect for lunch or a light dinner, offering sandwiches, salads, and a variety of baked goods, all made from scratch daily.

- **Specialty:** Don't miss their homemade soups and the turkey avocado sandwich, perfect for a fulfilling meal after a day of exploring.

Milt's Stage Stop (Cedar City)

- **Overview:** Milt's Stage Stop, situated on the outskirts of Cedar City on the way to Cedar Breaks, is an experience in itself. This rustic steakhouse, operating since 1956, offers meals in a log cabin that overlooks spectacular views of the Cedar Mountain.

- **Specialty:** Milt's is best known for its steaks and seafood. The ribeye steak and the deep-fried shrimp are local favorites.

Grind Coffee House (Cedar City)

- **Overview:** For those who start their day early or need a midday pick-me-up, Grind Coffee House offers some of the best coffee in the area, along with a selection of pastries and light bites.

- **Specialty:** Enjoy a handcrafted latte or a cold brew coffee along with one of their freshly made cinnamon rolls or a savory breakfast burrito.

These dining options provide not just meals but experiences that reflect the local culture and cuisine, allowing visitors to connect more deeply with the region surrounding Cedar Breaks National Monument.

Fish Springs National Wildlife Refuge

Fish Springs National Wildlife Refuge, nestled in the southern portion of Utah's Great Basin Desert, is a unique oasis characterized by its series of spring-fed wetlands. These lush wetlands contrast starkly with the arid desert surroundings, creating a vital habitat for a wide array of wildlife. The refuge covers approximately 17,992 acres and is a crucial stopover for migratory birds along the Pacific Flyway. The isolated nature of Fish Springs offers a tranquil retreat for nature lovers, bird watchers, and photographers seeking solace away from crowded hotspots.

Geological Features

The geological makeup of Fish Springs National Wildlife Refuge is as intriguing as its biological diversity. The area is fundamentally shaped by its position at the western edge of the Bonneville Basin. Over thousands of years, geological forces have sculpted a landscape characterized by deep playa deposits, extensive mud flats, and the distinctive marshlands that are fed by the Fish Springs Range.

The springs themselves are a remarkable feature, emerging from deep within the earth, possibly connected to the ancient Lake Bonneville. These springs provide a constant water source, creating a series of lush oases in the desert. The water chemistry of the springs is unique, containing high levels of dissolved minerals which contribute to the formation of unusual sedimentary deposits around the vent areas.

The refuge's terrain includes notable salt flats that border the wetland areas, where the evaporation of mineral-rich waters leaves behind vast, white expanses. These salt flats and the surrounding desert terrain offer starkly beautiful vistas, contrasting dramatically with the blue waters and greenery of the wetlands.

Historical Significance

Fish Springs National Wildlife Refuge holds a rich mosaic of human and natural history. Archaeological evidence suggests that Native American groups, including the Goshute tribe, utilized the Fish Springs area for thousands of years. The springs provided a rare and valuable water source in the desert, supporting the Native Americans and the diverse wildlife.

In the mid-19th century, the Fish Springs area became a site of interest during the exploration of the West. It was charted by the Simpson Expedition in 1859, which documented the springs and the unique flora and fauna of the area. Later, it served as a station for the Pony Express and the Overland Mail Service, playing a small but vital role in expanding communication and transportation across the United States.

Today, the refuge preserves the natural ecosystems and the history of human interaction with this challenging yet vibrant landscape, providing educational opportunities and a glimpse into the past through various artifacts and historical sites preserved within its boundaries.

Off-Peak Seasons

Visiting Fish Springs National Wildlife Refuge during the off-peak seasons offers a more solitary experience, ideal for those seeking to connect deeply with nature without the distraction of larger crowds.

- **Late Fall:** As temperatures begin to drop, visitor numbers dwindle, but the wildlife viewing remains exceptional. Waterfowl begin to migrate to the area, and the cooler weather makes exploring the diverse habitats more comfortable.

- **Winter:** The harsher winter conditions mean very few visitors brave the refuge. Those who do are rewarded with a serene, frost-laden landscape often enveloped in mists that rise from the warm springs into the cold air.

- **Early Spring:** Before the rush of spring birders arrives to witness the migratory spectacle, early spring offers a quiet interlude. The melting snow feeds into the wetlands, rejuvenating the aquatic ecosystems and attracting the first waves of returning birds.

Visiting during these quieter months allows for a more personal appreciation of Fish Springs' unique geological features, historical significance, and its critical role in regional biodiversity.

Weekday vs. Weekend Visits

Visiting Fish Springs National Wildlife Refuge during weekdays presents a unique opportunity to experience the serenity and natural beauty of the area without the interruption of larger crowds that are common on weekends. For those seeking peace and an undisturbed connection with nature, choosing a weekday to explore this secluded oasis can greatly enhance the experience.

Benefits of Weekday Visits:

- **Fewer Crowds:** Naturally, weekdays experience significantly fewer visitors, allowing for a more tranquil exploration of the refuge's diverse habitats. This solitude enhances the peacefulness of the environment and increases the likelihood of wildlife encounters as animals are less disturbed by human presence.

- **Unhurried Exploration:** With fewer visitors, you can take your time to wander through the refuge without feeling rushed or crowded. This is especially beneficial for photographers and nature enthusiasts who require time to observe their surroundings thoroughly.

- **Personal Interactions:** With less demand on their time, the refuge staff can provide more personalized attention, offering in-depth information and answering questions in more detail, which enriches your visit.

- **Enhanced Wildlife Viewing:** The quiet of a weekday visit means wildlife is more likely to be active throughout the day, improving opportunities for observation and photography.

Time of Day Strategies

The time of day can significantly impact what you see and experience at Fish Springs National Wildlife Refuge. Choosing when to visit can make your trip even more memorable, especially if you're keen on capturing the area's natural beauty or observing specific wildlife behaviors.

Early Morning Visits:

- **Advantages:** The early morning hours are magical at Fish Springs as the sun rises over the wetlands and the desert. Wildlife is typically more active during the cooler morning temperatures, making it an ideal time for bird watching and observing other animals as they start their day.

- **Experience:** Begin your visit with a tranquil morning walk along the springs, where you can enjoy the chorus of bird calls and perhaps catch a glimpse of mammals coming to drink from the springs.

Late Afternoon Visits:

- **Advantages:** Late afternoon brings a change in light and mood to the refuge. The setting sun paints the landscape in golden hues, and temperatures begin to cool, providing a comfortable setting for exploration.

- **Experience:** Trails like the one leading to the overlook points are less frequented in the late afternoon, offering a quiet and visually stunning hiking experience. This time is also excellent for photographers looking to capture the vibrant sunset skies reflected in the wetlands.

Exploring Lesser-Known Areas

Fish Springs National Wildlife Refuge boasts several lesser-known areas that offer remarkable experiences away from the main visitor paths. Exploring these areas provides a deeper understanding of the refuge's diverse ecosystems and landscapes.

Cathedral Valley:

- **Features:** Located within Capitol Reef National Park, Cathedral Valley is an accessible area from Fish Springs for a day trip. Known for its monolithic sandstone formations, this remote valley offers a starkly beautiful landscape that feels worlds apart from the wetlands of Fish Springs.

- **Experience:** The Cathedral Valley Loop Drive takes you through some of the most impressive formations, including the Temple of the Sun and Moon, providing a spectacular backdrop for photography and solitude.

The Waterpocket Fold:

- **Features:** Also near Capitol Reef, the Waterpocket Fold is a dramatic geologic feature extending from the park to Lake Powell. This area offers rugged trails and significant solitude.

- **Experience:** Exploring the Fold involves hiking through narrow canyons and expansive vistas that showcase the region's geological diversity. It's ideal for those looking to combine physical activity with geological exploration.

By visiting these lesser-known areas, you can escape even the smallest crowds and immerse yourself in the untouched beauty of Utah's high desert and rocky plateaus.

Wildlife Viewing and Nature Photography

Wildlife viewing and nature photography at Fish Springs National Wildlife Refuge can be profoundly rewarding experiences when conducted responsibly. Observing wildlife without causing disturbance is crucial for the animals' well-being and preserving their natural behaviors.

Best Practices for Observing Wildlife and Nature Photography:

- **Maintain a Respectful Distance:** Always keep a safe distance from wildlife to avoid stress and disruption to their natural activities. Use binoculars and telephoto lenses to observe or photograph from afar.

- **Stay on Trails:** Minimize your environmental impact by sticking to designated trails and observation points. This helps protect natural habitats and reduces the chances of disturbing wildlife.

- **Be Patient and Quiet:** Wildlife is more likely to be visible if you are quiet and patient. Sudden movements or loud noises can frighten animals away. Spend time quietly waiting, and the wildlife will often come to you.

- **No Feeding:** Feeding wildlife can alter their natural behaviors and diet, harming their health. Observe wildlife as they are and allow them to feed naturally.

- **Use Natural Light:** When photographing wildlife, rely on natural light as much as possible. Avoid using flash as it can startle animals, affecting their eyesight and behavior.

- **Educate Yourself:** Before visiting, learn about the wildlife species you will likely encounter. Understanding their behavior and needs can enhance your experience and reduce the likelihood of causing disturbance.

By following these guidelines, visitors can ensure their wildlife viewing and photography do not negatively impact the natural environment or its inhabitants.

Stargazing Opportunities

Fish Springs National Wildlife Refuge offers exceptional stargazing opportunities due to its isolated location and minimal light pollution. Here are some tips for enjoying the night sky in these ideal stargazing conditions:

Tips for Stargazing:

- **Plan Around the Moon:** For the best stargazing experience, plan your visit during a new moon when the sky is darkest. Avoid nights when the moon is full, as the moonlight can wash out fainter stars.

- **Bring the Right Equipment:** A simple pair of binoculars or a small telescope can enhance your view of the stars, planets, and other celestial objects.

- **Use Red Light Flashlights:** To preserve your night vision, use flashlights with red filters. This helps ensure your eyes adjust to the dark and remain sensitive to subtle light variations in the sky.

- **Dress Appropriately:** Nights in the desert can be cold, even in summer. Bring warm clothing and a blanket or chair during long stargazing sessions.

- **Choose an Open Spot:** Find an open area in the refuge away from any remaining light sources. The ponds at Fish Springs can reflect the night sky, adding to the beauty of your stargazing experience.

Where to Stay

When visiting Fish Springs National Wildlife Refuge, consider staying in nearby towns to avoid crowds and enhance your experience of the area.

Torrey:

- **Overview:** Located about an hour and a half from Fish Springs, Torrey offers a range of lodging options, from motels and bed and breakfasts to cabins.

- **Accommodations:** Options like the Capitol Reef Resort or the Cougar Ridge Lodge offer comfortable stays with beautiful scenic views of the surrounding landscapes.

Delta:

- **Overview:** To the north of Fish Springs, Delta provides basic amenities and lodging choices, which include hotels and inns that cater to a variety of budgets.

- **Accommodations:** The Days Inn by Wyndham Delta offers straightforward, comfortable lodging, and it's an excellent base for exploring the northern parts of the wildlife refuge.

Fillmore:

- **Overview:** East of Fish Springs, Fillmore offers various services and accommodations. It's an excellent choice for visitors coming from the eastern routes.

- **Accommodations:** The Best Western Paradise Inn and Resort in Fillmore provides a more full-service option, with dining and recreational facilities on site.

Staying in these nearby towns gives you more choices, allows you to explore the local communities, and allows you to enjoy the peaceful rural charm of the areas surrounding Fish Springs National Wildlife Refuge.

Dining Recommendations

While Fish Springs National Wildlife Refuge is somewhat remote, several nearby towns offer delightful dining options that escape the usual tourist crowds. These local eateries provide a taste of authentic Western cuisine and a glimpse into the area's culinary culture. Here are some recommended spots where you can enjoy a meal that feels genuinely local:

Delta:

- **El Jalisciense Mexican Restaurant:** A local favorite, El Jalisciense serves up authentic Mexican dishes in a friendly, casual setting. Known for its generous portions and fresh flavors, it's a great spot to refuel after a day at the refuge.

- **The Rancher Café:** Offering classic American diner fare, The Rancher Café is perfect for those looking for a hearty breakfast or a homemade pie. It's a local gathering place, so it's also a good spot to get insights into hidden gems in the area.

Fillmore:

- **Cluff's Car Hop Cafe:** Step back in time at Cluff's Car Hop Cafe, a vintage-style diner that offers burgers, shakes, and all the classics. It's not just about the food here; it's about experiencing a slice of Americana with friendly service.

- **Garden of Eat'n:** This quaint spot is perfect for those looking for something lighter or health-conscious. Offering a variety of salads, wraps, and vegetarian options, Garden of Eat'n caters to a diverse palate.

Torrey:

- **Slackers Burger Joint:** Located in the scenic town of Torrey, Slackers is known for its burgers, fries, and a selection of local beers. It's a casual spot perfect for unwinding after a day of hiking or bird-watching.

- **Café Diablo:** For a more upscale dining experience, Café Diablo offers innovative Southwestern cuisine in a vibrant, art-filled setting. The restaurant's use of local ingredients and creative dishes make it a must-visit for foodies.

Beaver:

- **Crazy Cow Café:** Located in Beaver, about two hours from Fish Springs, this family-owned café is well-known for its home-style cooking and warm, welcoming atmosphere. The Crazy Cow Café offers everything from breakfast classics to steaks and seafood.

- **Timberline Inn Restaurant:** For a slightly more formal dining option in Beaver, the Timberline Inn Restaurant provides a cozy dining experience with various American classics, specializing in steak and seafood.

These dining options provide delicious meals, allow guests to engage with the local community, and allow them to enjoy the hospitality that rural Utah is known for.

Goblin Valley State Park

Goblin Valley State Park, nestled in the heart of Utah's red rock country, offers a surreal landscape unlike any other in the world. Known for its thousands of hoodoos and mushroom-shaped rock pinnacles, referred to as "goblins," this park provides a fascinating, almost otherworldly vista that feels more like Mars than Earth. The valley's unique scenery is a playground for hikers, photographers, and families alike, offering a glimpse into a natural world of whimsical formations that inspire imagination and wonder.

Geological Features

Goblin Valley State Park is renowned for its extensive collection of sedimentary rock formations, sculpted over millions of years by water and wind erosion forces. The park is in a large basin bordered by the San Rafael Swell in the northeast, the Henry Mountains to the southeast, and the sprawling desert on all sides.

The "goblins" for which the park is named are technically known as hoodoos—tall, thin spires of rock that protrude from the bottom of arid basins. However, the goblins in Goblin Valley are unusually shaped, resembling mushrooms or misshapen heads, creating an eerie feel to the landscape. These formations are composed primarily of Entrada Sandstone, which layers different consistencies of sediment deposits along with hematite and geothite that contribute to the varied red, orange, and brown hues visible in the park.

Over time, the softer sandstone beneath the hard rock caps has eroded in irregular patterns, creating rows of these unique formations. This erosion process is ongoing, which means that the landscape of Goblin Valley is ever-changing, continually morphing into new and interesting shapes.

Historical Significance

Goblin Valley State Park's history is as rich and varied as its landscapes. Native American cultures, particularly the Fremont people, once roamed these lands, utilizing the vast resources offered by the desert environment. The area surrounding Goblin Valley is scattered with rock art and archaeological sites that date back thousands of years, providing insight into the lives of these early inhabitants.

The valley was relatively unknown to the wider world until the late 1920s when a few cowboys chasing cattle stumbled upon it. The area was designated a state park in 1964 to protect its fragile geological wonders. It has since become a favorite location for filmmakers looking for extraterrestrial-like settings, notably featured in the 1999 sci-fi film "Galaxy Quest."

Off-Peak Seasons

The best time to visit Goblin Valley State Park to avoid the crowds is during the off-peak seasons, which include late fall, winter, and early spring.

- **Late Fall:** The temperatures cool down, making it more comfortable to explore the park. The lower visitor numbers make it easier to enjoy the silence and solitude among the goblins.

- **Winter:** Snow rarely falls in Goblin Valley, but the cooler temperatures discourage most casual tourists. Those who do visit during winter will find a quiet, stark landscape.

- **Early Spring:** Before the spring break crowds arrive, early spring offers mild weather and manageable visitor numbers. It's a perfect time to photograph the park with a backdrop of occasional wildflowers blooming in the warmer patches.

Visiting during these times allows for a more introspective journey through this ancient landscape, where the silence and space amplify the visual impact of the goblins' eerie formations.

Weekday vs. Weekend Visits

Visiting Goblin Valley State Park during weekdays presents a distinct advantage for those looking to escape the crowds and enjoy the park's natural beauty in solitude. Opting for a weekday visit can significantly enhance the experience by offering a quieter environment, which is beneficial for exploring and relaxing.

Benefits of Weekday Visits:

- **Reduced Crowds:** One of the most noticeable benefits of visiting on a weekday is the significant crowd reduction. This makes parking and navigating the park easier and enhances the experience by preserving the tranquility of the natural setting.

- **Unhindered Access to Popular Spots:** With fewer people around, visitors have better access to the most sought-after areas and formations without waiting or navigating through groups of tourists.

- **More Interaction with Park Staff:** Fewer visitors means more opportunities for personalized interactions with park rangers and staff, who can offer in-depth knowledge and interesting anecdotes about the park's geology and history.

- **Ideal for Photography:** Photographers will find weekdays particularly appealing, as they can take their time setting up shots without interruption and capture the park's landscapes under varying natural light conditions without working around crowds.

Time of Day Strategies

Choosing the right time of day to visit Goblin Valley can drastically impact your experience, especially in terms of lighting and temperature, which are critical in desert environments like this.

Early Morning Visits:

- **Advantages:** The early morning is one of the best times to visit Goblin Valley. The light at sunrise illuminates the rock formations spectacularly, casting long shadows and highlighting the textures of the goblins. Temperatures are also cooler, making hikes more comfortable.

- **Experience:** Start your day with a sunrise viewing from the Observation Point, followed by a hike on the Entrada Canyon Trail while the light is still soft and the temperatures are mild.

Late Afternoon Visits:

- **Advantages:** The late afternoon light brings a different quality to the landscape, with warmer tones and softer shadows. As the day cools down, late afternoons are perfect for exploring without the harsh midday sun.

- **Experience:** Plan your visit to include sunset, which can be stunning as the setting sun paints the valley in vibrant reds and oranges. The Goblin's Lair and the Carmel Canyon Loop are spectacular during this time.

Exploring Lesser-Known Areas

While Goblin Valley is famous for its main valley of hoodoos, the park also offers lesser-known areas that provide a sense of discovery and isolation away from the more frequented paths.

Exploring the Periphery:

- **Features:** Beyond the central valley, the park's periphery trails, such as the Wild Horse Mesa and Molly's Castle, provide expansive views of the surrounding terrain and less traffic, allowing for a more meditative experience.

- **Experience:** These areas are ideal for longer hikes and offer a different perspective of the park's landscape, showcasing the vastness and variety of the surrounding desert.

Canyoneering Adventures:

- **Features:** For those seeking a more adventurous experience, canyoneering routes in Goblin Valley offer a thrilling way to explore the park's hidden slots and gorges. Little Wild Horse Canyon and Bell Canyon are popular among canyoneers for their accessible yet challenging routes.

- **Experience:** These canyons offer a physical challenge and a unique way to experience the park's geological wonders, often leading to secluded areas that the average visitor rarely sees.

Exploring these lesser-known areas adds to the adventure and provides a deeper appreciation for the park's extensive natural beauty, away from the main tourist spots.

Sample Itineraries for Crowded Days

Visiting Goblin Valley State Park on crowded days requires a strategic approach to maximize your enjoyment while avoiding the most congested areas. Here's how to structure your visit:

Early Morning: Beat the Crowds

- **Activity:** Arrive at the park just as it opens, typically around sunrise. Begin your day with a hike on the Goblin's Lair Trail, which is less popular than the Three Sisters but just as impressive. This early start takes advantage of the cooler morning temperatures and means fewer people on the trails.

- **Highlight:** Capture the morning light on the unique formations, providing excellent photography opportunities with fewer photo bombs.

Mid-Morning: Explore Lesser-Known Features

- **Activity:** As the main valley starts to fill up, head to the Observation Point or embark on the Entrada Canyon Trail, both of which tend to be less crowded. These areas offer beautiful views and a quieter experience.

- **Highlight:** Enjoy the solitude and the expansive scenery that allows for personal reflection and leisurely exploration.

Lunchtime: Picnic Off the Beaten Path

- **Activity:** Pack a picnic lunch and head towards the Curtis Bench area. This area offers picnic tables with incredible views and usually has fewer visitors during peak lunch hours.

- **Highlight:** Relax with a meal in a peaceful setting, away from the park's busier central areas.

Afternoon: Valley Floor Exploration

- **Activity:** As some morning visitors begin to leave, venture into the heart of the valley where the iconic goblins are located. Later in the afternoon, you can sometimes see a decrease in crowd sizes.

- **Highlight:** Walk among the goblins, and if you're feeling adventurous, participate in some casual rock scrambling.

Late Afternoon: Sunset Views

- **Activity:** Conclude your day with a sunset view from the Carmel Canyon Loop, offering less foot traffic and stunning sunset colors over the valley.

- **Highlight:** Experience the changing colors of the landscape as the sun sets, providing a perfect end to your day.

Flexible Itinerary Ideas

Having a flexible itinerary at Goblin Valley State Park allows you to adapt to varying crowd levels and still enjoy a fulfilling visit:

High Crowd Levels:

- **Morning:** Start with the least crowded trails, like the Entrada Canyon or Curtis Bench.

- **Afternoon:** If the walking paths are too crowded, visit the park's educational exhibits or consider a scenic drive around the area.

Moderate Crowd Levels:

- **Explore Mid-Morning:** Head to moderately visited sites early, then enjoy the main attractions like Goblin Valley floor mid-afternoon when early visitors may start to leave.

- **Late Afternoon:** Enjoy activities like photography or leisurely walks at observation points.

Low Crowd Levels:

- **Take Advantage:** With fewer visitors, explore the most popular areas like the Three Sisters and the heart of Goblin Valley. Engage in longer hikes or more thorough exploration of the area.

Off-the-Beaten-Path Hikes

For those looking to escape even the smallest crowds, exploring off-the-beaten-path hikes in and around Goblin Valley offers a more solitary and intimate interaction with the landscape.

Cassidy Arch Trail:

- **Location:** This trail is not in Goblin Valley itself but in the nearby Capitol Reef National Park. It offers a rigorous hike with rewarding views of the stunning Cassidy Arch.

- **Experience:** The trail is less frequented due to its difficulty and length, making it a great option for those seeking solitude and adventure.

Wild Horse Window:

- **Features:** This lesser-known gem is a short hike leading to a spectacular natural window formed by erosion. It offers picturesque views and a quiet spot to appreciate the park's rugged beauty.

- **Experience:** The trail to Wild Horse Window is less traveled and provides a peaceful hike suitable for contemplative exploration and excellent photographic opportunities.

These trails are perfect for visitors looking for unique experiences away from the main tourist spots. They allow for deeper exploration and enjoyment of the area's natural wonders.

Wildlife Viewing and Nature Photography

Goblin Valley State Park offers a unique wildlife viewing and photography opportunity, given its distinct desert ecosystem. To ensure a respectful interaction with the wildlife and to capture the natural beauty without causing harm, consider the following best practices:

- **Maintain Distance:** Always keep a respectful distance from any wildlife you encounter. When photographing wildlife, use zoom lenses to avoid getting too close, which can stress the animals.

- **Minimize Noise:** Move quietly and speak softly when observing wildlife. Sudden noises can startle animals, causing them stress and potentially forcing them to leave their habitat.

- **Use Natural Light:** When photographing, use natural light to avoid using flash, which can disorient animals, especially at twilight or nighttime.

- **Stay on Trails:** Keep to designated paths to minimize your impact on the natural environment and avoid disturbing wildlife in their natural habitats.

- **Patience is Key:** Good wildlife viewing and photography often require patience. Wait quietly, and animals will be more likely to appear.

- **No Feeding:** Feeding wildlife can alter their natural behaviors and diet, which can be harmful to their health and well-being.

By adhering to these guidelines, visitors can enjoy and capture the park's natural wonders in a way that is safe and sustainable for the wildlife that calls it home.

Stargazing Opportunities

Goblin Valley State Park is renowned for its dark skies, making it an ideal spot for stargazing. Here are some tips to enhance your night sky viewing experience in this remote location:

- **Plan Around the Moon:** Check the lunar calendar and plan your visit during the new moon for the darkest skies and best stargazing conditions. Avoid full moon nights when the moonlight can wash out dimmer stars.

- **Use Red Light Flashlights:** To preserve night vision, use flashlights with red bulbs when navigating dark. This helps ensure that your eyes adjust more effectively to low-light conditions.

- **Arrive Early:** Allow your eyes at least 30 minutes to adapt to the dark before starting your stargazing session. This will help you see more stars and make the experience more rewarding.

- **Bring the Right Equipment:** A simple pair of binoculars can greatly enhance your view of the night sky, allowing you to see more details on the moon, planets, and deep-sky objects like galaxies and nebulae.

- **Seek Out Open Areas:** Areas like the observation point above the valley offer expansive sky views with minimal obstruction. These spots are perfect for setting up telescopes or relaxing and enjoying the sprawling Milky Way.

Where to Stay

While Goblin Valley State Park has limited on-site accommodation, several nearby towns offer a range of lodging options that can enhance your visit without the crowds. Consider these alternatives:

- **Green River:** Located about 45 minutes north of the park, Green River offers various motels and hotels that cater to all budgets. It's a convenient base for exploring Goblin Valley and other nearby attractions.

- **Hanksville:** A small town about 30 minutes south of the park, Hanksville provides a quieter alternative for lodging. It has a few motels and is close enough for early-morning trips to the park or late-night stargazing.

- **Torrey:** Approximately an hour west of Goblin Valley, Torrey is known for its proximity to Capitol Reef National Park and offers more upscale lodging options. It's ideal for visitors looking to combine their trip with other scenic locations.

Staying in these towns helps avoid crowds, supports local economies, and provides a more immersive experience of Utah's beautiful and diverse desert landscape.

Dining Recommendations

While Goblin Valley State Park itself is remote and doesn't offer dining options, the surrounding areas provide a variety of local eateries that serve as delightful stops for those venturing through Utah's red rock country. These less touristy local dining spots give visitors a taste of authentic local flavors and a slice of small-town hospitality.

Green River, Utah

- **Ray's Tavern:** A beloved institution in Green River, Ray's Tavern is known for its no-frills, down-to-earth atmosphere and delicious, hearty meals. Specializing in burgers and steaks grilled to perfection, it's a favorite among locals and visitors alike. The friendly service and community vibe make it a must-visit for anyone passing through.

- **Tamarisk Restaurant:** Located on the banks of the Green River, Tamarisk Restaurant offers diners tasty American and Southwestern cuisine and scenic views of the river. Their patio is a lovely spot for a meal after a day of exploring, especially during sunset.

Hanksville, Utah

- **Duke's Slickrock Grill:** Hanksville's own Duke's Slickrock Grill serves up a menu full of hearty, comforting dishes that reflect the local cuisine. With its Western-themed decor and friendly service, Duke's offers a warm welcome to tired travelers looking for a substantial meal.

- **Blondie's Eatery & Gift:** Known for its casual dining atmosphere, Blondie's provides a simple yet satisfying selection of American classics, perfect for refueling before or after visiting Goblin Valley. It's also a great spot to pick up locally-made gifts and souvenirs.

Torrey, Utah

- **Café Diablo:** For those willing to drive a little further, Café Diablo in Torrey offers a creative take on Southwestern cuisine with a menu that features local ingredients and innovative dishes. The restaurant's unique art-filled environment and excellent service make it a memorable dining experience.

- **Capitol Reef Inn & Cafe:** This cozy establishment offers both a cozy inn and a café. It serves homemade meals with a touch of local charm. The café is particularly noted for its pies, which are made with fresh, local fruit.

Boulder, Utah

- **Hell's Backbone Grill & Farm:** Located in the small town of Boulder, Hell's Backbone Grill offers a unique dining experience with its organic, locally sourced ingredients and farm-to-table approach. The restaurant adheres to Buddhist principles, emphasizing sustainable and ethical food production and preparation, making it a standout dining destination in southern Utah.

Each of these eateries provides not just nourishment but also a taste of the local culture, making them perfect complements to your exploration of Goblin Valley and the surrounding landscape.

Snow Canyon State Park

Snow Canyon State Park, nestled in the stunning red rock country of southwestern Utah near St. George, offers a dramatic landscape of jagged canyons, lava flows, and delicate sandstone cliffs. Named not for seasonal snowfall but for early Utah leaders Lorenzo and Erastus Snow, the park features a diverse range of vibrant geological formations and a variety of plant and animal life, making it a lesser-known gem compared to Utah's larger national parks.

Geological Features

Snow Canyon State Park showcases the dynamic geological processes that have shaped the Colorado Plateau. The park's landscape is dominated by Navajo sandstone, which has been eroded by wind and water over millions of years to reveal layers of red and white rock that create a striking visual contrast against the blue skies.

Key geological features of the park include:

- **Petrified Dunes:** These are ancient sand dunes that have turned to rock, capturing a moment in time and displaying beautiful cross-bedding caused by wind patterns.

- **Lava Tubes:** The park is dotted with extinct cinder cones and lava tubes, remnants of the volcanic activity that once shaped this land. Visitors can explore several tubes where lava once flowed beneath the surface.

- **Jagged Canyons:** The park's canyons, such as Jenny's Canyon (a narrow slot canyon), provide dramatic evidence of the powerful forces of erosion. These canyons offer cool, shaded hikes which are a relief in the desert heat.

Each of these features tells a story of environmental change and resilience, offering visitors a unique opportunity to walk through living history and experience the raw power of Earth's geological forces.

Historical Significance

Snow Canyon's history is deeply entwined with the Native American tribes, particularly the Ancestral Puebloans and Paiute tribes, who inhabited the area for thousands of years. The park's landscape provided these communities with essential resources, from the rich plant life used for food and medicine to the rocky outcrops utilized for shelter and defense.

In the 19th century, Mormon pioneers entered the region. The park's modern name honors Lorenzo Snow, a prominent Mormon leader. During the early 20th century, the area served as a backdrop for several Hollywood films, including Westerns and historical epics, which brought a different kind of notoriety to the stunning landscape.

Off-Peak Seasons

The best times to visit Snow Canyon State Park to avoid the crowds are during the off-peak seasons of late fall, winter, and early spring.

- **Late Fall:** Temperatures cool, making it perfect for hiking and exploring. The park's flora transitions, and the lower visitor numbers create a serene hiking experience.

- **Winter:** Mild winter temperatures and the possibility of light snow create a stunning contrast with the red rock, providing exceptional photographic opportunities. The park is quiet, offering a peaceful escape.

- **Early Spring:** Before the heat and crowds of summer, spring brings a burst of life to the park, with wildflowers beginning to bloom and wildlife becoming more active. This season is ideal for those looking to experience the park's natural beauty with minimal disturbance.

Visiting during these times allows for a more intimate connection with the park's breathtaking landscapes and rich history, providing a tranquil and enriching outdoor experience.

Weekday vs. Weekend Visits

Choosing to visit Snow Canyon State Park on weekdays instead of weekends can significantly enhance the quality of your experience, allowing you to enjoy the park's stunning landscapes and tranquil atmosphere without the crowds.

Benefits of Weekday Visits:

- **Fewer Crowds:** Weekdays see significantly fewer visitors, which means less noise and congestion on the trails and at popular viewpoints. This allows for a more relaxed and personal connection with nature.

- **Enhanced Wildlife Sightings:** With fewer people and less disturbance, wildlife is more likely to be visible during the weekdays. Animals that might be hidden during busy weekend periods can often be spotted in their natural habitats.

- **No Waiting Times:** Many popular spots within the park can become bottlenecked with visitors on weekends. Visiting on a weekday usually means no waiting for parking spots, quicker access to trails, and more freedom to explore at your own pace.

- **Better Interaction With Park Staff:** With fewer visitors to attend to, park staff can provide more personalized attention, offer more detailed information, and engage more with individual visitors, enhancing your understanding and enjoyment of the park.

Time of Day Strategies

The time of day you choose to explore Snow Canyon State Park can greatly impact your experience, especially in terms of lighting, temperature, and crowd levels.

Early Morning Visits:

- **Advantages:** The early morning light enhances the beauty of the red rock formations and makes for cooler hiking conditions. It is also the best time to take photographs with soft, diffused light.

- **Experience:** Hiking trails such as the Butterfly Trail and Petrified Dunes are particularly stunning in the morning light. Early risers are also more likely to encounter wildlife that retreats during the hotter parts of the day.

Late Afternoon Visits:

- **Advantages:** Later in the day, the setting sun casts a golden hue on the sandstone, which is ideal for photography. Temperatures begin to cool, making hikes more comfortable.

- **Experience:** Trails like the Johnson Canyon Trail, which is often shaded in the afternoon, offer a pleasant hike with the added bonus of experiencing the changing light conditions that transform the landscape.

Exploring Lesser-Known Areas

Snow Canyon State Park has its popular spots, but many lesser-known areas offer equally stunning scenery without the crowds. Exploring these areas can lead to a more solitary and unique experience.

Cinder Cone Trail:

- **Features:** This trail offers a moderate hike to a volcanic cinder cone, providing a different perspective of the park's geological diversity. It's less frequented but offers panoramic views of the surrounding desert and volcanic terrain.

- **Experience:** Cinder Cone Trail's solitude is perfect for those seeking quiet reflection away from busier areas.

Whiterocks Amphitheater:

- **Features:** Located off the beaten path, Whiterocks Amphitheater is a limestone bowl that contrasts sharply with the more common red sandstone formations.

- **Experience:** Accessible via a less-known trail, this area is ideal for peaceful hiking and enjoying the dramatic landscape with minimal disturbance.

By visiting during off-peak times, whether it's choosing weekdays over weekends or selecting the optimal times of day, and by exploring lesser-known trails, you can maximize your enjoyment of Snow Canyon State Park. Each visit can offer a new perspective and appreciation for this dynamic and beautiful natural area.

Sample Itineraries for Crowded Days

When visiting Snow Canyon State Park during crowded days, structuring your itinerary to avoid peak areas can greatly enhance your experience. Here's a planned day that minimizes interaction with large groups:

Early Morning: Pioneer Names Trail

- **Activity:** Start with the Pioneer Names Trail early in the morning. This short and easy trail is close to the entrance and allows you to view historic names painted on the rock walls from the 1800s. Its proximity to the entrance and quick completion time means you can enjoy it before larger crowds arrive.

- **Highlight:** Catch the early morning light, which enhances the visibility of the names and provides cooler walking conditions.

Mid-Morning: Petrified Dunes Trail

- **Activity:** Head to the Petrified Dunes Trail as morning progresses. These ancient sand dunes turned into stone offer a fantastic landscape for exploration and photography.

- **Highlight:** The trail offers multiple vantage points for views of the park, ideal for photography before the sun is too high.

Lunch: Picnic at Upper Galoot Picnic Area

- **Activity:** Enjoy a packed lunch at one of the picnic areas, ideally Upper Galoot, which is less crowded than others. This time allows for a rest and recharge before continuing your day.

- **Highlight:** Use this quieter time for wildlife watching, as many animals are active before the heat of the day sets in.

Afternoon: Butterfly Trail

- **Activity:** In the afternoon, when the park is at its busiest, take the Butterfly Trail, which is often less crowded than more central trails. This trail offers beautiful natural scenery and a chance to see the park's diverse plant life.

- **Highlight:** The trail's shaded areas provide relief from the afternoon sun, making your hike more comfortable.

Late Afternoon: Lava Flow Overlook

- **Activity:** End your day with a visit to the Lava Flow Overlook, a short walk leading to a stunning view of an ancient lava field. By this time, earlier crowds tend to diminish.

- **Highlight:** The setting sun casts beautiful shadows over the lava fields, creating perfect photography opportunities.

Flexible Itinerary Ideas

Flexibility in your plans can help you adapt to varying crowd levels at Snow Canyon State Park:

High Crowd Levels:

- **Morning:** Tackle the more remote or challenging trails early in the day, like the Hidden Pinyon Trail.

- **Afternoon:** Visit the interpretive center or enjoy less frequented overlooks like the West Canyon Overlook.

Moderate Crowd Levels:

- **Explore all day:** Mix popular spots with less-visited areas, adjusting your locations based on real-time observations of where visitors are congregating.

Low Crowd Levels:

- **Take Full Advantage:** Explore the park's most popular trails and sites like Jenny's Canyon and the Sand Dunes, enjoying the lack of usual visitor numbers.

Off-the-Beaten-Path Hikes

For those looking for solitude and natural beauty, off-the-beaten-path hikes in Snow Canyon provide a peaceful alternative to the more frequented trails:

Cassidy Arch Trail:

- **Location:** This trail is not in Snow Canyon but in nearby Capitol Reef National Park. It offers a rigorous hike to a beautiful natural arch, avoiding the heavy traffic of more popular trails in Snow Canyon.

- **Experience:** The hike is moderately challenging, deterring some casual visitors, which helps maintain a quieter environment.

Whiptail Trail:

- **Features:** This paved trail is suitable for all ages and activity levels and is excellent for cycling or a leisurely walk, often less crowded than other areas.

- **Experience:** Enjoy the stunning canyon scenery with fewer interruptions, making it perfect for a peaceful day out.

Exploring these trails offers physical benefits and the chance to connect more deeply with the park's diverse landscapes away from the crowds.

Wildlife Viewing and Nature Photography

Observing wildlife and capturing the natural beauty of Snow Canyon State Park can be rewarding experiences, provided they are done responsibly to ensure minimal disturbance to the environment and its inhabitants.

Best Practices for Wildlife Viewing and Nature Photography:

- **Maintain a Safe Distance:** Always keep a safe and respectful distance from wildlife. Use binoculars for viewing and long lenses for photography to minimize stress on the animals.

- **Move Slowly and Quietly:** Quick movements and loud noises can frighten wildlife. Move slowly and speak quietly to increase your chances of observing natural behaviors.

- **Use Natural Light:** Whenever possible, use natural light to avoid startling wildlife with flash photography. The soft light of early morning or late afternoon is ideal for both animal comfort and photographic quality.

- **Stay on Designated Paths:** Straying from trails can damage fragile habitats and disturb wildlife. Stick to established paths to protect the environment and maintain the natural behavior of the park's animal residents.

- **Be Patient:** Good wildlife viewing and photography often require patience. Animals may take time to reappear after initially being spotted. Waiting quietly and respectfully can lead to rewarding encounters.

- **Respect the Environment:** Take care to leave no trace of your visit. Avoid altering or damaging their natural surroundings, which includes not feeding wildlife or interfering with their activities.

By following these guidelines, visitors can enjoy observing and photographing wildlife without negatively impacting their natural behaviors or habitats.

Stargazing Opportunities

Snow Canyon State Park offers spectacular stargazing opportunities thanks to its remote location and minimal light pollution. Here are tips for making the most of your night sky viewing experience:

Planning Your Visit:

- **Check the Lunar Calendar:** Plan your stargazing around the new moon phase for the darkest skies. Full moon nights, while beautiful, can wash out dimmer stars.

- **Arrive Early:** Allow your eyes to adjust to the darkness. It typically takes about 20-30 minutes for your eyes to adapt to night conditions fully.

- **Bring Appropriate Gear:** A star map or a stargazing app can enhance your experience. Binoculars or a small telescope can also help you see celestial objects more clearly.

- **Use Red Lights:** If you need light, use a flashlight with a red filter or a red LED. Red light interferes less with night vision than white light.

Choosing Your Spot:

- **Find an Open Area:** Open areas away from trees and high walls will provide an unobstructed view of the sky. The park's dunes area is a good option.

- **Minimize Light Pollution:** Even within the park, aim to position yourself away from any park lights or the glow from nearby towns.

Where to Stay

For those visiting Snow Canyon State Park and looking to avoid crowds, staying in smaller towns nearby can offer a more secluded base:

St. George:

While St. George is relatively larger and busier, it offers a wide range of lodging options, from budget motels to upscale hotels. Staying on the outskirts can provide easier access to the park while avoiding the downtown crowds.

Ivins:

Just outside Snow Canyon, Ivins is a small town with limited but charming accommodation options. It provides quick access to the park and a quiet, scenic environment.

Santa Clara:

A short drive from Snow Canyon, Santa Clara offers a small selection of lodgings in a peaceful, residential setting. It's close enough for easy park access but far enough to avoid large groups of tourists.

Torrey:

Although farther away, Torrey is a quiet option for those also planning to visit Capitol Reef National Park. It provides a range of accommodations, from rustic cabins to comfortable inns, suitable for a quieter, nature-focused visit.

Choosing to stay in these areas helps avoid crowds and supports local communities and enhances the overall experience of your trip with a touch of local flavor and hospitality.

Dining Recommendations

When visiting Snow Canyon State Park, the surrounding towns offer a selection of dining options that capture the local flavor without the typical tourist crowds. Here are some highly recommended eateries where you can enjoy delicious meals and a taste of local hospitality after a day of exploring the park:

St. George:

- **Cliffside Restaurant:** Perched on a cliff overlooking the city and its surroundings, Cliffside Restaurant offers stunning views and a menu of contemporary American cuisine that focuses on fresh, local ingredients. The patio seating is particularly popular for sunset dinners.

- **Painted Pony Restaurant:** Located in the historic district of St. George, the Painted Pony brings a touch of elegance to the dining scene with its sophisticated menu that includes locally sourced meats and seasonal specialties. It's a great spot for a relaxing dinner after a day of hiking.

Santa Clara:

- **Ka'ili's:** For those craving a taste of the Pacific, Ka'ili's offers exquisite Polynesian-inspired dishes in a laid-back atmosphere. It's a family-run spot that provides a warm welcome and flavors that are hard to find elsewhere in the area.

- **The Granary Café:** Located in a historic granary, this quaint café serves up farm-to-table fare with a focus on organic ingredients. The menu changes seasonally, reflecting the best of what's local and fresh.

Ivins:

- **Aragosta Restaurant:** Known for its fine dining experience, Aragosta offers a menu primarily based on seafood and steak options crafted with an international flair. The chef's attention to detail and the intimate setting make it ideal for a special evening out.

- **Xetava Gardens Café:** Nestled in the Kayenta Art Village, Xetava Gardens Café provides a tranquil dining experience with a menu that includes creative dishes made from local ingredients. The outdoor seating surrounded by desert art and sculptures offers a unique ambiance.

Springdale (nearby Zion National Park):

- **Oscar's Café:** Just a short drive from Snow Canyon, Oscar's Café in Springdale is beloved for its hearty portions and vibrant atmosphere. Their menu features Mexican and American favorites, perfect for refueling after a long hike.

- **Bit & Spur Restaurant and Saloon:** Offering Mexican-inspired cuisine with a Utah twist, Bit & Spur uses fresh, local ingredients to craft its flavorful dishes. The restaurant also features a selection of local craft beers and a lively environment.

Each of these dining spots provides not just meals but experiences that reflect the local culture and cuisine, making them perfect stops during your visit to Snow Canyon State Park and the surrounding areas.

The Wave (Coyote Buttes North)

The Wave, located in the Coyote Buttes North area of the Paria Canyon-Vermilion Cliffs Wilderness on the Arizona-Utah border, is a dazzling, undulating rock formation renowned for its striking, wave-like structure and brilliant, swirling patterns of red and yellow sandstone. Access to this geological marvel is highly coveted, managed through a competitive lottery system to preserve its delicate beauty. Its remote location and hiking difficulty add to its allure, making it a pilgrimage site for serious hikers and photographers from around the world.

Geological Features

The Wave is primarily made up of Jurassic-age Navajo Sandstone, approximately 190 million years old. The layers of sandstone have been compacted and then slowly eroded by wind and rain, carving out the intricate ripples and troughs that give the formation its name. The landscape is characterized by its smooth, undulating surfaces, and the cross-bedding of the rock layers is visible in the sharp and sweeping lines that curve through the formation, creating an illusion of movement.

The rock's color variations, ranging from reds to yellows, are due to iron oxide pigments within the layers. The differential erosion of the softer and harder layers contributes to the surreal, wave-like appearance. The Wave also includes several small rock arches, honeycombed holes, and other fascinating erosional forms, making it a geological treasure trove.

Historical Significance

While The Wave is not known for its rich historical human presence like other areas in the Southwest, it holds a significant place in modern cultural heritage as an iconic subject of contemporary nature photography. Its discovery and subsequent popularity in the late 20th century paralleled the rise of landscape photography as a major genre of art, and images of The Wave have become almost emblematic of the American Southwest's wild, untouched landscapes.

The area around Coyote Buttes North has been traversed by various Native American tribes over centuries, including the Navajo, who have longstanding cultural ties to the land. The wilderness around The Wave remains largely untouched by modern development, preserving its pristine condition and the sense of timelessness that many visitors seek.

Off-Peak Seasons

The best time to visit The Wave is during the off-peak seasons of late fall, winter, and early spring, when you can avoid the crowds and increase your chances of winning a permit in the lottery system.

- **Late Fall:** Conditions are ideal as the temperature cools, making hiking more pleasant. The softer light of autumn enhances the photographic appeal of the sandstone's colors.

- **Winter:** Despite shorter days and the potential for cold weather, winter visits offer a rare chance to see The Wave with light dustings of snow, contrasting dramatically with the red rock. Visitor numbers drop significantly, increasing permit availability.

- **Early Spring:** Before the rush of spring break crowds and the intense heat of summer, early spring can provide a sweet spot with moderate temperatures and fewer competitors for permits.

Visiting during these months increases your chances of securing a permit and offers a more solitary experience in this extraordinary landscape. It allows for personal reflection and appreciation of one of nature's most impressive artworks.

Weekday vs. Weekend Visits

Visiting The Wave (Coyote Buttes North) or any popular natural landmark during weekdays instead of weekends can significantly enhance the quality of the experience due to reduced crowds. For The Wave, where access is already strictly limited by a permit system, choosing a weekday to visit can further ensure a more serene and personal experience.

Benefits of Weekday Visits:

- **Enhanced Solitude:** With fewer visitors overall, weekdays offer a quieter environment, allowing for more intimate encounters with the natural landscape.

- **Increased Flexibility:** Fewer visitors can mean more freedom to explore at your own pace without feeling hurried or constrained by the presence of large groups.

- **Better Interaction with Nature:** A less crowded setting enhances the likelihood of wildlife sightings and provides a peaceful atmosphere for enjoying the natural sounds and vistas.

- **Improved Photographic Opportunities:** With fewer people, photographers can take their time to set up and capture the perfect shot without interruptions or waiting for clear views.

Time of Day Strategies

Choosing the right time of day to visit popular trails like The Wave can greatly affect your viewing experience, impacting everything from photography to personal comfort.

Early Morning Visits:

- **Advantages:** Morning light offers cooler hiking temperatures and casts a magical glow on the rock formations, enhancing their colors and contours. The sun's angle in the morning can dramatically highlight the wave-like patterns and provide deep, elongated shadows for stunning photographic effects.

- **Experience:** Start your hike early to take full advantage of the solitude and light. Morning is also an excellent time for wildlife activity, as many desert creatures are nocturnal and may be seen returning to their resting places.

Late Afternoon Visits:

- **Advantages:** Afternoon light warms the colors of the rock, giving the landscape a vibrant hue that is dramatically different from the morning. As the sun sets, the changing light can offer a new perspective on The Wave, with golden tones and softer shadows.

- **Experience:** Hiking later allows for potentially less crowded trails as morning visitors depart. The late afternoon is also perfect for those wanting to capture sunset photography, where the interplay of light and shadow can create a mesmerizing visual landscape.

Exploring Lesser-Known Areas

The area surrounding The Wave also offers several lesser-known trails and viewpoints that can provide a more secluded experience away from the main attraction:

Cathedral Valley:

- **Features:** Located in Capitol Reef National Park, Cathedral Valley is known for its monolithic sandstone formations, which are similar in their dramatic appearance to The Wave but attract fewer visitors.

- **Experience:** Explore trails like the Cathedral Valley Loop, which offers a full-day driving adventure with occasional hikes to impressive overlooks and formations.

Waterpocket Fold:

- **Features:** This dramatic geologic feature in Capitol Reef offers a range of hiking and exploration opportunities along its 100-mile spine. It is less frequented than more accessible areas of the park.

- **Experience:** Venture down less-traveled paths like the Burro Wash or the Cottonwood Wash, which provide solitude and unique geological insights and photogenic spots.

Exploring these areas diversifies your visit and allows for personal discovery and appreciation of the region's diverse landscapes, often in complete solitude. Each offers unique geological features and scenic beauty that can rival the main attractions but without the same level of foot traffic.

Sample Itineraries for Crowded Days

When visiting popular natural attractions like The Wave on crowded days, careful planning can help you avoid the busiest areas and make the most of your experience. Here's a sample itinerary designed to optimize your visit:

Early Start: The Wave Hike

- **Activity:** Start your day early by hitting the trail to The Wave at sunrise. This allows you to enjoy the cool morning air and experience the area with as few people as possible. Capture the early morning light that enhances the vibrant colors and dramatic curves of The Wave.

- **Highlight:** Utilize the soft morning light for photography, which is often ideal for highlighting the intricate patterns and deep colors of the rock formations.

Mid-Morning: Second Wave

- **Activity:** As the main wave area starts to fill up, head to the second wave or other nearby but less frequent formations. Though slightly less famous, these areas still offer stunning rock formations and a quieter experience.

- **Highlight:** The Second Wave offers similar dramatic landscapes but typically attracts fewer visitors, allowing for a more relaxed exploration.

Lunch Break: Picnic Off the Beaten Path

- **Activity:** Enjoy a picnic lunch in a secluded spot. Areas north of The Wave or along the Cottonwood Canyon Road offer scenic views and less foot traffic.

- **Highlight:** Find a quiet spot with natural shade to relax and refuel before continuing your adventure.

Afternoon: Sidestep to Other Attractions

- **Activity:** In the afternoon, when the sun is at its peak and the main attractions are most crowded, take a short drive to other nearby sights. Consider visiting other parts of the Vermilion Cliffs or exploring the Paria River area.

- **Highlight:** These areas provide a sense of solitude and unique landscapes without the crowds found at The Wave.

Flexible Itinerary Ideas

Flexibility is key when exploring areas known for their popularity and beauty. Here are some strategies based on varying crowd levels:

High Crowd Levels:

- **Morning:** Tackle the most popular sights early when crowd levels are at their lowest.

- **Afternoon:** Explore lesser-known areas or nearby attractions as crowds peak at popular spots.

Moderate Crowd Levels:

- **Adjust on the Fly:** Monitor crowd levels at popular spots and be ready to change your plan. If an area is too crowded, have backup options ready in nearby less crowded regions.

Low Crowd Levels:

- **Take Full Advantage:** With fewer visitors, explore the most popular trails and landmarks at your leisure. This is a rare opportunity to enjoy big attractions with minimal interruption.

Off-the-Beaten-Path Hikes

For those willing to explore beyond the main trails, here are suggestions for less frequented but equally stunning hikes:

Cassidy Arch Trail:

- **Location:** Located in Capitol Reef National Park, this trail is a fantastic alternative to more crowded sites. The trail leads to an impressive natural arch set against striking rock formations.

- **Experience:** While it requires a moderate hike, Cassidy Arch Trail is often less crowded, offering a more serene hiking experience and excellent photo opportunities without the rush.

Wire Pass to Buckskin Gulch:

- **Features:** A slot canyon that rivals the more famous Antelope Canyon, this hike offers an immersive experience into deep narrow canyons with ancient rock walls.

- **Experience:** This trail has fewer visitors than The Wave and provides a profound sense of isolation and awe.

By exploring these alternative trails and using a flexible approach to your itinerary, you can greatly enhance your experience, avoiding the busiest spots while still enjoying the breathtaking landscapes that this region has to offer.

Wildlife Viewing and Nature Photography

Observing wildlife and capturing the natural beauty of environments like The Wave requires consideration and respect for the natural habitat and its inhabitants. Here are best practices for wildlife viewing and nature photography that ensure minimal disturbance:

- **Keep Your Distance:** Always maintain a respectful distance from wildlife. Use a good pair of binoculars or a telephoto lens for close-up shots to avoid stressing animals.

- **Move Slowly and Quietly:** Wildlife is easily startled by loud noises and sudden movements. Move slowly and quietly to increase your chances of observing natural behaviors.

- **Use Natural Light:** To prevent disturbing animals, especially during sensitive times such as dusk and dawn, utilize natural light for photography. Avoid using flash, which can disorient and scare wildlife.

- **Stay on Trails:** Follow designated paths to minimize your impact on the natural environment. Straying off the trail can destroy habitats and disturb wildlife unnecessarily.

- **Be Patient:** Great wildlife observations and photography opportunities often come to those who wait. Spend time quietly observing your surroundings, and the wildlife will often reappear after initial disturbances.

- **Respect the Rules:** Adhere to all local guidelines and regulations regarding wildlife interaction and photography. These rules are designed to protect both the animals and their environment.

Stargazing Opportunities

The Wave and its surrounding areas offer some of the darkest night skies, making them perfect for stargazing. Here's how to maximize your experience under the stars:

- **Check the Lunar Calendar:** Plan your stargazing around the new moon phase when the sky is darkest. Full moons, while beautiful, can illuminate the sky and obscure fainter stars and galaxies.

- **Bring the Right Equipment:** A star map or stargazing app can help you identify constellations and celestial events. A telescope or a pair of binoculars can enhance your viewing experience, bringing distant stars and planets into clearer view.

- **Use Red Light Flashlights:** Preserve your night vision by using flashlights with red bulbs. Red light minimizes the impact on your ability to see the stars.

- **Choose Open Spaces:** Open areas away from tall formations like those around The Wave will provide unobstructed views of the night sky. Avoid areas with light pollution from nearby cities or facilities.

- **Dress Appropriately:** Nights in the desert can be cold, especially outside of the summer months. Bring warm clothing and blankets to ensure a comfortable stargazing experience.

Where to Stay

To avoid crowds and enhance your experience near The Wave, consider staying in smaller, nearby towns that offer a range of accommodations:

- **Page, Arizona:** About a two-hour drive from The Wave, Page offers a variety of hotels and guesthouses. It's a convenient base for exploring other attractions like Lake Powell and Antelope Canyon.

- **Kanab, Utah:** Closer than Page, Kanab is about an hour from The Wave and offers numerous lodging options, from motels to bed and breakfasts. It's a charming town with access to multiple natural attractions in the area.

- **Torrey, Utah:** While a bit further away, staying in Torrey gives you access to The Wave and to Capitol Reef National Park. It offers a variety of accommodations, including hotels, inns, and guesthouses.

Choosing to stay in these areas allows for a more relaxed visit, away from the larger crowds that can accumulate in more popular tourist hubs. Each location provides its unique charm and range of services, making your trip both enjoyable and convenient.

Dining Recommendations

When visiting The Wave and the surrounding regions, dining at local eateries that cater more to residents than tourists can enhance your travel experience, providing authentic flavors and a taste of the local culture. Here are some recommended spots in nearby towns that offer delicious meals without the typical tourist crowds:

Page, Arizona:

- **BirdHouse**: Offering a quirky and cozy dining atmosphere, BirdHouse is known for its delicious fried chicken and homemade sides. It's a favorite among locals for its comfort food and friendly service.

- **Big John's Texas BBQ**: For a taste of authentic Texas barbecue in the desert, Big John's Texas BBQ is a must-visit. Located in an outdoor setting with picnic tables and live music, this spot is popular for its smoked meats and laid-back vibe.

Kanab, Utah:

- **Rocking V Cafe**: Known for its eclectic menu and art gallery setting, Rocking V Cafe serves dishes made from fresh, locally sourced ingredients. The menu features a variety of options, from gourmet burgers to creative vegetarian dishes.

- **Peekaboo Canyon Wood Fired Kitchen**: This vegetarian restaurant is a gem in Kanab. It offers wood-fired pizzas, fresh salads, and a selection of craft beers and wines. The ambiance is casual and welcoming, with a focus on sustainable dining.

Torrey, Utah:

- **Slackers Burger Joint**: Located in the heart of Torrey, Slackers offers a variety of burgers, sandwiches, and shakes in a relaxed, diner-style atmosphere. It's a great place to refuel after a day of hiking.

- **Café Diablo**: Café Diablo provides a unique dining experience with its innovative Southwestern cuisine made from local ingredients. The restaurant's creative dishes, such as rattlesnake cakes, are complemented by its vibrant, art-filled decor.

Springdale, Utah:

- **Oscar's Cafe**: Just outside Zion National Park, Oscar's Cafe offers hearty meals in a lively setting. Known for its Mexican-inspired breakfasts and dinners, it's a great spot to start or end your day in the area.

- **Bit & Spur Restaurant and Saloon**: Featuring Mexican and Southwestern cuisine, Bit & Spur offers a large selection of craft beers and a friendly atmosphere. Their spacious patio is perfect for enjoying a meal under the stars.

These dining options provide not just nourishment but also an opportunity to engage with the local community. Each establishment reflects the unique charm of its town, ensuring that your meals are memorable parts of your travel experience.

Kodachrome Basin State Park

Kodachrome Basin State Park, nestled in southern Utah, is famed for its strikingly colorful and uniquely shaped rock formations. Named after the iconic Kodachrome film by National Geographic photographers who visited the area in 1948, the park captivates visitors with its vivid landscape that blends rich hues and geological marvels. The park spans approximately 2,240 acres and is renowned for its monolithic spires, which rise majestically from the valley floor and vary in color from creamy whites to deep reds.

Geological Features

Kodachrome Basin State Park is distinguished by its array of geologic structures, most notably the sedimentary pipes or spires that dominate the landscape. Over 67 monolithic stone spires are found throughout the park, some reaching as high as 170 feet. These spires are believed to be the solidified remnants of ancient geysers or springs that were once active in the area, where minerals and sediments accumulated over thousands of years, forming these distinctive columns.

The park also showcases a variety of other geological formations, including massive sandstone layers, arches, and various erosional features. The Chimney Rock and Shakespeare Arch are notable landmarks, each offering unique perspectives on the forces of erosion and sediment deposition that have shaped this land over millennia. The colorful sandstone layers, rich in iron oxide pigments, provide breathtaking views, especially during sunrise and sunset when the rocks appear to glow with intense warmth.

Historical Significance

While the Kodachrome Basin does not have a long history of human settlement, it has a rich cultural heritage associated with Native American tribes, particularly the Paiute and Fremont people, who roamed these lands. The park's name, bestowed in 1962, reflects the mid-20th century enthusiasm for the vibrant, color-saturated Kodachrome film, which was revolutionary in bringing the American West's vivid colors to life in photography.

The park was explored more thoroughly during the 1940s when it was "rediscovered" by National Geographic Society expedition teams. Their photographic work within the park led to its naming and eventual designation as a state park in 1963, ensuring the preservation of its unique geological and natural features.

Off-Peak Seasons

Visiting Kodachrome Basin State Park during the off-peak seasons can significantly enhance the experience, as there are fewer visitors and more favorable conditions for exploration.

- **Late Fall:** The temperatures cool, making hiking and photography more comfortable and enjoyable. The lower visitor numbers make it easier to appreciate the park's solitude and natural beauty.

- **Winter:** Mild winter weather in this region makes it a perfect time for those seeking tranquility. Occasional snowfall contrasts beautifully against the red rock formations, offering unique photographic opportunities.

- **Early Spring:** Before the rush of the summer crowds, early spring sees the park come alive with blooming wildflowers and active wildlife under typically mild weather conditions.

Visiting during these times allows for a more leisurely and intimate exploration of Kodachrome Basin's stunning landscapes, making it ideal for those seeking both adventure and solitude in the great outdoors.

Weekday vs. Weekend Visits

Choosing to visit Kodachrome Basin State Park on weekdays rather than weekends can significantly enhance the visitor experience, primarily due to reduced crowd sizes. Here are some of the key benefits of opting for a weekday visit:

- **Reduced Crowds:** Fewer visitors are present on weekdays, providing a more solitary experience. This allows for uninterrupted hikes and the opportunity to enjoy the natural sounds and sights of the park without the disturbance of large groups.

- **Greater Access to Popular Sites:** With fewer people, access to the most popular sites and trails becomes easier. This means less time waiting for parking spots, scenic viewpoints, and photographic opportunities, allowing for a smoother and more enjoyable visit.

- **More Wildlife Sightings:** Wildlife tends to be more active and visible when there are fewer humans around. Weekday visitors often report more frequent wildlife encounters because animals are less disturbed by humans' presence.

- **Enhanced Interaction with Park Staff:** Fewer visitors means that park staff can provide more personalized attention. This could include detailed explanations at visitor centers, guided tours, and personalized recommendations for hiking routes.

Time of Day Strategies

The time of day can greatly influence your experience at Kodachrome Basin State Park, especially on busier days. Here's how to optimize early morning and late afternoon visits:

Early Morning Visits:

- **Advantages:** The early morning light is ideal for photography, enhancing the reds and oranges of the rock formations. It also offers cooler hiking temperatures. Additionally, mornings typically see fewer visitors, allowing for a more peaceful start to the day.

- **Experience:** The morning hours are perfect for tackling longer trails such as the Angel's Palace Trail, where the soft morning light offers a magical view of the park's vast landscape.

Late Afternoon Visits:

- **Advantages:** Late afternoon into sunset is another prime time for photographers as the setting sun casts dramatic shadows and lights up the spires and columns with a golden glow. Temperatures begin to cool, making hikes more comfortable.

- **Experience:** Trails like the Shakespeare Arch and Sentinel Trail offer stunning sunset views, where the low sun accentuates the textured surfaces of the rock formations.

Exploring Lesser-Known Areas

While Kodachrome Basin is famous for its spires and colorful rock formations, several lesser-known areas within and near the park also offer remarkable landscapes with fewer visitors:

Cathedral Valley:

- **Features:** Located in the northern section of nearby Capitol Reef National Park, Cathedral Valley is known for its monolithic sandstone formations that resemble cathedrals. This area is remote and less trafficked, offering a sense of vast wilderness and isolation.

- **Experience:** Exploring Cathedral Valley involves a challenging loop drive that is best navigated with a high-clearance vehicle, making it an adventure for those seeking off-the-beaten-path experiences.

Waterpocket Fold:

- **Features:** This dramatic geologic feature also in Capitol Reef offers a lengthy north-to-south trek through varied terrain, from rugged canyons to striking rock layers.

- **Experience:** Hiking or driving the length of the Waterpocket Fold, especially the southern portions, provides a deep dive into the area's geological diversity without the crowds typical of more accessible park areas.

By planning visits during weekdays, leveraging the optimal times of day, and venturing into less-explored areas, visitors can fully appreciate the unique beauty and solitude of Kodachrome Basin State Park and its surroundings.

Sample Itineraries for Crowded Days

Visiting Kodachrome Basin State Park during peak days requires strategic planning to enjoy the park fully while avoiding the most crowded areas. Here's how to structure your visit:

Early Start: Grand Parade Trail

- **Activity:** Begin your day early by hiking the Grand Parade Trail, which is less traveled than the park's more central attractions. This trail offers beautiful views and gentle terrain, making it suitable for morning light photography and peaceful walks.

- **Highlight:** Capture the sunrise colors on the rock formations, and enjoy bird watching as the day begins.

Mid-Morning: Angel's Palace Trail

- **Activity:** As the crowds start to gather at more accessible spots, head to Angel's Palace Trail. This moderately easy trail offers panoramic views and fascinating rock structures, usually with fewer visitors.

- **Highlight:** The trail provides excellent opportunities for photography from elevated vantage points, showcasing the vast array of spires and columns.

Lunch: Picnic at Basin

- **Activity:** Enjoy a packed lunch at one of the picnic areas in the park, chosen for its scenic views and less traffic. This break will also allow you to wait out the peak midday crowds.

- **Highlight:** Use this time to relax under natural shade, observe the natural flora and fauna, or simply enjoy the quiet.

Afternoon: Nature Center and Gift Shop

- **Activity:** Visit the park's nature center and gift shop in the afternoon when it is hotter and more people are taking shelter. This is a great time to learn about the park's geological history and pick up souvenirs.

- **Highlight:** Engage with park staff to learn more about the lesser-known facts of Kodachrome Basin and get tips for future visits.

Late Afternoon: Shakespeare Arch

- **Activity:** As the day cools down, take a hike to Shakespeare Arch. This lesser-visited site offers a beautiful natural arch, and the late afternoon light enhances its impressive structure.

- **Highlight:** Enjoy the cooler part of the day in a tranquil setting, perfect for winding down your visit.

Flexible Itinerary Ideas

Flexibility in your visit can help you navigate fluctuating crowd levels effectively. Here are some strategies:

High Crowd Levels:

- **Explore Early or Late:** Hit the trails early in the morning or later in the evening, when most visitors are less likely to be active.

- **Alternate Attractions:** If the main attractions are crowded, explore lesser-known areas or trails off the main route.

Moderate Crowd Levels:

- **Dynamic Planning:** Monitor crowd movements. If a popular spot seems overwhelming, head to your next planned location and circle back when it might be quieter.

Low Crowd Levels:

- **Take Your Time:** With fewer crowds, explore at a leisurely pace. Spend more time at each site, take more photos, or sit and appreciate the natural beauty around you.

Off-the-Beaten-Path Hikes

For those looking for solitude and unique landscapes, Kodachrome Basin offers some off-the-beaten-path hikes:

Cassidy Arch Trail:

- **Location:** Located in Capitol Reef National Park, this trail is a bit of a drive from Kodachrome but offers stunning views and a thrilling hike to a beautiful arch set in the red rock.

- **Experience:** Though more challenging, this hike rewards with fewer visitors and spectacular photo opportunities.

Cool Cave:

- **Features:** Not as well-known, Cool Cave is accessible via a moderate hike that offers interesting rock formations and, often, much-needed shade.

- **Experience:** This spot is ideal for those looking to explore more quietly and escape the typical paths trodden by most park visitors.

These options provide quieter alternatives to the park's busier areas, perfect for visitors seeking a more intimate connection with nature.

Wildlife Viewing and Nature Photography

Observing wildlife and capturing the natural beauty of areas like Kodachrome Basin State Park requires mindfulness and respect for the environment. Here are some best practices for wildlife viewing and nature photography:

- **Maintain a Safe Distance:** Always keep a respectful distance from wildlife. Use binoculars for viewing and telephoto lenses for photography. This ensures that animals are not disturbed by human presence.

- **Move Quietly and Slowly:** Avoid sudden movements and loud noises that can startle wildlife. Moving slowly and quietly increases your chances of observing animals in their natural behaviors.

- **Use Natural Light:** To minimize the impact on wildlife, utilize natural light for photography. Avoid using flash, which can disorient animals, especially during twilight and nighttime.

- **Stay on Designated Paths:** Sticking to trails and public areas helps protect natural habitats, reduce stress on wildlife, and prevent the destruction of native flora.

- **Be Patient. Patience is key in wildlife viewing and photography. Once disturbed, animals may take time to reappear**. Wait quietly, and you might be rewarded with a unique sighting.

- **Respect the Environment:** Do not attempt to feed or bait wildlife as this can alter natural behaviors and potentially harm their health. Preserve the naturalness of the environment by leaving no trace of your visit.

Stargazing Opportunities

Kodachrome Basin State Park offers exceptional stargazing opportunities due to its remote location and minimal light pollution. Here are some tips to enhance your stargazing experience:

- **Plan for New Moon Phases:** The best time for stargazing is during a new moon when the sky is darkest. Check lunar calendars and plan your visit around these periods for optimal star visibility.

- **Use Red Light Flashlights:** Use red light flashlights to preserve your night vision. Red lights are less disruptive to both human eyes and wildlife, making it easier to adjust to the darkness while navigating.

- **Bring Appropriate Equipment:** Binoculars or a telescope can enhance your stargazing experience by bringing distant celestial objects into view.

- **Choose Open Areas:** Open areas away from trees and high terrain offer the best views of the sky. The Grand Parade area within Kodachrome Basin is particularly suitable for unobstructed night sky viewing.

- **Dress Accordingly:** Nighttime temperatures can drop significantly, especially outside of summer months. Dress warmly to ensure comfort during your stargazing session.

Where to Stay

To avoid crowds and enhance your experience near Kodachrome Basin State Park, consider staying in smaller, nearby towns which offer a range of accommodations:

Cannonville:

Located just a few miles from the park, Cannonville is a quieter alternative to larger towns. It offers several cozy bed and breakfasts and campgrounds.

Tropic:

Tropic provides a range of lodging options, from motels to cabins, and it's only about ten minutes away from the park. It's a great base to explore Kodachrome and Bryce Canyon National Park, which is nearby.

Bryce Canyon City:

For those looking to stay close to more amenities while still accessing the park, Bryce Canyon City offers several larger hotels and resorts.

Torrey:

Although a bit further, staying in Torrey provides access to Kodachrome Basin and to Capitol Reef National Park. It offers a variety of accommodations, including hotels, inns, and guesthouses, suitable for a quieter, nature-focused visit.

Staying in these areas allows for a more relaxed visit, away from the larger crowds that can accumulate in more popular tourist hubs. Each location provides its unique charm and range of services, making your trip both enjoyable and convenient.

Dining Recommendations

Exploring Kodachrome Basin State Park provides the perfect opportunity also to taste the local flavors of the surrounding southern Utah area. Dining at local eateries that cater more to residents than to tourists can enhance your travel experience, offering authentic meals and a taste of local culture. Here are some top dining options in the nearby towns that provide delicious meals without the typical tourist crowds:

Cannonville:

- **Stone Hearth Grille:** Nestled slightly off the beaten path, this grille offers a fine dining experience with a focus on local ingredients and a menu that changes seasonally. The setting is intimate, and the views of the surrounding landscape add a special touch to the dining experience.

- **Cannonville Cafe:** A simple, no-frills diner that serves up hearty, home-cooked meals perfect for fueling a day of hiking and exploration. Known for its friendly service, it's a great spot to mingle with locals.

Tropic:

- **IDK Barbecue:** Celebrated for serving some of the best BBQs in the area, IDK Barbecue is a must-visit in Tropic. The casual atmosphere and focus on high-quality, smoked meats make it a favorite among both locals and savvy visitors.

- **The Rustler's Restaurant:** Located in the Bryce Pioneer Village, The Rustler's Restaurant offers a range of American classics and comfort foods with a homey feel. It's a good place to enjoy a satisfying breakfast or dinner in a rustic setting.

Bryce Canyon City:

- **Ebenezer's Barn and Grill:** Offering a unique dining experience, Ebenezer's serves traditional Western fare in a barn-themed venue with live country music. While it caters to tourists, it provides a fun cultural experience that captures the spirit of the Old West.

- **Ruby's Inn Cowboy's Buffet and Steak Room:** Known for its hearty breakfasts and western-style dinners, Ruby's Inn offers a variety of dishes that cater to all tastes, making it ideal for families and large groups.

Escalante:

- **Escalante Outfitters Cafe:** A favorite among hikers and local adventurers, this cafe serves delicious pizzas, sandwiches, and salads. It's also a great spot for gathering local hiking tips and stories from fellow diners.

- **Circle D Eatery:** Known for its friendly atmosphere and comfort food, Circle D Eatery offers a range of dishes from burgers and steaks to vegetarian options, all prepared with a homestyle touch.

These eateries provide nourishment and an opportunity to engage with the local community, offering insights into the area's culinary culture.

Little Wild Horse Canyon

Little Wild Horse Canyon, nestled in the heart of Utah's San Rafael Swell, is a premier destination for slot canyon enthusiasts. Renowned for its accessible and family-friendly slot canyon hikes, this area offers a captivating adventure through winding, narrow passageways formed by the relentless forces of water erosion. The canyon's smooth and undulating sandstone walls, towering high above the canyon floor, create a surreal and otherworldly landscape that is both awe-inspiring and exhilarating to explore.

Geological Features

Little Wild Horse Canyon is a classic example of slot canyon topography. Its narrow, deep channels cut into the Navajo Sandstone, predominantly through the mechanical erosion from flash flooding. The canyon walls, often only a few feet apart, soar to heights of 100 feet or more, creating dramatic corridors beneath a sliver of sky. These corridors showcase a collage of geological history, with layers of sandstone that vary in color from creamy whites to deep reds, each layer telling a story of ancient environments that ranged from deserts to seas.

The smooth walls of the canyon feature a myriad of wave-like patterns, chutes, and hollows, sculpted by wind and water over millions of years. The lower sections of Little Wild Horse Canyon are particularly sculptured, offering hikers an intimate experience with these natural forces, where at points, they can touch both sides of the canyon with outstretched arms.

Historical Significance

The area surrounding Little Wild Horse Canyon has been a significant landscape in the history of the indigenous peoples of the Colorado Plateau, including the Fremont culture and later the Southern Paiute tribes. The canyon and its environs are rich in archaeological significance, with numerous rock art panels and ancient dwellings that provide insight into the lives of these early inhabitants.

In more recent history, the canyon has become a symbol of Utah's wild and untamed beauty, attracting photographers, hikers, and nature lovers drawn by its natural beauty and relative accessibility. It has also played a part in the broader conservation and outdoor recreation movements in the Southwest, illustrating the ongoing American value placed on wilderness and natural landscapes.

Off-Peak Seasons

The best time to visit Little Wild Horse Canyon to avoid the crowds and experience the solitude of the canyons is during the off-peak seasons:

- **Late Fall:** Cooler temperatures make hiking more comfortable, and the reduced likelihood of flash floods makes exploring the narrow passages safer.

- **Winter:** Although colder, winter visits can offer a quiet and starkly beautiful experience, with fewer visitors and the chance of light snow dusting the canyon walls, highlighting their contours.

- **Early Spring:** Before the onset of the busier spring and summer months, early spring can be ideal, with moderate temperatures and the occasional wildflower beginning to bloom along the trail edges.

Visiting during these times ensures a more peaceful experience, allowing for personal reflection and a deeper connection with Little Wild Horse Canyon's ancient and dynamic landscape.

Weekday vs. Weekend Visits

Choosing to visit Little Wild Horse Canyon on weekdays rather than weekends can significantly enhance the quality of your experience due to decreased visitor numbers. Here are some advantages to planning a weekday visit:

- **Reduced Crowds:** Weekdays generally see fewer visitors, which translates into a more serene hiking experience. You'll encounter fewer groups on the trails, allowing you to enjoy the natural sounds and sights without interruptions.

- **Better Access to Popular Spots:** With fewer people around, you'll have better access to the most popular segments of the canyon. This means less waiting time to navigate through narrow passageways and more opportunity to take uninterrupted photos.

- **More Wildlife Sightings:** Wildlife tends to be more active and less elusive on quieter days. On weekdays, you're more likely to encounter native birds and wildlife that might stay hidden during busier weekend visits.

- **Enhanced Interaction with Nature:** Fewer visitors mean a quieter environment and a more impactful personal interaction with the landscape. You'll be able to appreciate the intricate details of the canyon's geology and take in the vastness of the area without the distraction of large crowds.

Time of Day Strategies

The time of day you choose to explore Little Wild Horse Canyon can dramatically affect your experience, especially during peak visitor seasons. Here's how to optimize early morning and late afternoon visits:

Early Morning Visits:

- **Advantages:** The early morning is ideal for visiting slot canyons like Little Wild Horse. Cooler temperatures make for a comfortable hike, and the morning light illuminates the canyon walls, enhancing the red and orange hues.

- **Experience:** Starting your hike at sunrise helps you beat the heat and the crowds. Early morning light is perfect for photography, offering soft, diffused lighting that highlights the textures of the canyon walls.

Late Afternoon Visits:

- **Advantages:** Late afternoon offers another sweet spot for canyon exploration. The setting sun casts long shadows and paints the sandstone walls in vibrant colors, creating a dramatic backdrop for photographers.

- **Experience:** Hiking during the late afternoon also means you'll likely be exiting the canyon as most visitors are leaving, giving you a quieter descent and possibly the chance to enjoy sunset views in solitude.

Exploring Lesser-Known Areas

For those looking to avoid the popular paths and explore quieter areas of Little Wild Horse Canyon and its surroundings, consider these lesser-known gems:

Cathedral Valley:

- **Features:** Located in Capitol Reef National Park, Cathedral Valley is known for its monolithic sandstone formations that resemble cathedrals. Far less trafficked than more accessible park areas, it offers a remote wilderness experience.

- **Experience:** Accessing Cathedral Valley involves a rugged loop drive that is best navigated with a high-clearance vehicle. It offers a day-long adventure through some of Capitol Reef's most stunning backcountry.

Waterpocket Fold:

- **Features:** Also in Capitol Reef, the Waterpocket Fold extends from the north to the south of the park and features a diverse landscape of cliffs, canyons, and domes.

- **Experience:** Exploring lesser-known trails like the Burro Wash and Cottonwood Wash can provide solitude and the opportunity to view rock formations and natural arches without the crowds typical of the park's more frequented areas.

These strategies for visiting during off-peak times and exploring less popular areas can help you fully enjoy Little Wild Horse Canyon and the surrounding regions, enhancing your overall experience with these spectacular natural landscapes.

Sample Itineraries for Crowded Days

Planning a visit to Little Wild Horse Canyon on a crowded day requires a strategy to optimize your experience while avoiding the most congested areas. Here's a structured itinerary to help manage your day:

Early Morning: Start at Little Wild Horse Canyon

- **Activity:** Begin your hike early in the morning to take advantage of fewer crowds and cooler temperatures. Starting early also means better lighting for photography within the narrow canyon walls.

- **Highlight:** Enjoy the tranquility and the morning light which beautifully highlights the sinuous rock walls, creating a photogenic environment.

Mid-Morning: Explore Bell Canyon

- **Activity:** As Little Wild Horse Canyon starts to fill up, switch to Bell Canyon, which often receives fewer visitors and offers equally stunning rock formations and narrower slots.

- **Highlight:** Bell Canyon provides a different perspective and variety of formations, offering a quieter hike as most crowds stick to the more famous Little Wild Horse.

Lunch Break: Goblin Valley State Park

- **Activity:** For a midday break, head over to nearby Goblin Valley State Park. Use this time to have lunch and explore the unique geological formations resembling goblins.

- **Highlight:** The park's open area allows you to stretch out and relax away from the narrower canyon confines, and you can enjoy a picnic with a view.

Afternoon: Return or Extend Hike

- **Activity:** Depending on the crowd levels, you might choose to extend your hike further into Bell Canyon or return to explore deeper parts of Little Wild Horse as some morning hikers start to leave.

- **Highlight:** Later in the day, the light changes, offering new perspectives and photography opportunities in different parts of the canyons.

Flexible Itinerary Ideas

Flexibility can greatly enhance your experience at Little Wild Horse Canyon, especially when dealing with varying crowd levels. Here are some adaptable strategies:

High Crowd Levels:

- **Alternate Plan:** If the canyons become too crowded, consider exploring nearby trails or scenic spots outside the immediate area, such as driving to the Wedge Overlook for expansive views of the Little Grand Canyon.

Moderate Crowd Levels:

- **Adapt as Needed:** Monitor the flow of people and adjust your hike timing accordingly. If the main canyon is busy, start with Bell Canyon and check Little Wild Horse later in the day.

Low Crowd Levels:

- **Explore Thoroughly:** Take advantage of the rare low crowds to explore both canyons more thoroughly, including side slots and possibly extending to connected hikes.

Off-the-Beaten-Path Hikes

For those seeking solitude and unique scenery, consider these lesser-known hikes:

Cassidy Arch Trail:

- **Location:** Situated in Capitol Reef National Park, this trail leads to an impressive natural arch set against a backdrop of striking Navajo Sandstone.

- **Experience:** The trail is moderately strenuous but offers solitude and stunning views, making the effort worthwhile.

Chute Canyon:

- **Features:** Part of the San Rafael Swell, Chute Canyon offers a less visited but equally captivating slot canyon experience adjacent to Little Wild Horse.

- **Experience:** Its remoteness and similar geological features provide a peaceful alternative, perfect for those looking to escape the popular routes.

These suggestions offer a balance of adventure and solitude, allowing for a full and enriching visit even on the busiest days at Little Wild Horse Canyon and surrounding areas.

Wildlife Viewing and Nature Photography

Observing wildlife and engaging in nature photography requires an approach that respects the natural environment and minimizes human impact. Here are some best practices:

- **Keep a Respectful Distance:** Always maintain a safe distance from wildlife to avoid causing stress or altering their natural behaviors. Use zoom lenses to capture close-up images without getting too close.

- **Move Slowly and Quietly:** Sudden movements and loud noises can startle animals. Move slowly and speak softly to increase your chances of observing wildlife without disturbing them.

- **Use Natural Light:** Use natural light as much as possible for photography. Avoid using flash, which can disrupt animals' natural rhythms and behaviors, especially during dawn and dusk, when many species are most active.

- **Stay on Trails:** Keep to designated paths to minimize your impact on the environment. This helps preserve habitats and reduces the chances of disturbing wildlife.

- **Be Patient:** Wildlife viewing often requires patience. Wait quietly, and give animals time to reappear after any disturbances.

- **Do Not Feed Wildlife:** Feeding animals can alter their natural foraging behaviors and potentially endanger their health. Keep all food secured and dispose of all waste properly.

Stargazing Opportunities

Little Wild Horse Canyon and the surrounding areas, with their remote locations and minimal light pollution, offer exceptional stargazing opportunities. Here are some tips to enhance your night-sky viewing experience:

- **Check the Lunar Calendar:** For the darkest skies, plan your stargazing around the new moon phase. Light from a full moon can wash out dimmer stars and celestial objects.

- **Use Red Light Flashlights:** Use flashlights with red filters to preserve your night vision and minimize disturbance to others when navigating or reading star maps at night.

- **Bring Appropriate Gear:** A telescope or binoculars can greatly enhance your view of celestial events, stars, and planets. Also, consider bringing a comfortable chair or a blanket to lie on.

- **Choose Open Areas:** Look for open spaces that offer unobstructed views of the sky. Avoid areas with tall structures or heavy tree cover.

- **Dress Appropriately:** Nights can be cold, especially outside of the summer months. Dress in layers to stay warm during nighttime viewing.

Where to Stay

To avoid crowds and enhance your experience near Little Wild Horse Canyon, consider staying in smaller, nearby towns that offer convenient access to the park and other local attractions:

- **Green River:** Located approximately an hour's drive from Little Wild Horse Canyon, Green River offers various hotel options and is well-positioned for exploring other nearby geological features and parks.

- **Torrey:** Approximately an hour and a half away, Torrey offers a range of accommodations, from motels to bed and breakfasts, and has access to Little Wild Horse Canyon and Capitol Reef National Park.

- **Hanksville:** A small town about 30 minutes from the canyon, Hanksville offers basic lodging options, perfect for those looking to stay close to their adventure without the bustle of larger towns.

- **Moab:** Although further away, Moab is an excellent base for those looking to explore a wider range of outdoor activities in the region, including Arches and Canyonlands National Parks. It offers a wide range of lodging, from luxury resorts to campgrounds.

Choosing to stay in these areas can provide a quieter, more intimate experience. You can enjoy both the day's adventures and the night's celestial displays without the crowds found in more tourist-heavy locations.

Dining Recommendations

When exploring areas around Little Wild Horse Canyon and the broader San Rafael Swell, dining at local, lesser-known eateries can enrich your travel experience with authentic regional flavors and a break from the typical tourist spots. Here are some recommended dining options in nearby towns that offer great food and local charm:

Green River, Utah:

- **Tamarisk Restaurant:** Located right on the banks of the Green River, Tamarisk Restaurant offers scenic views accompanied by a diverse menu that includes everything from traditional American dishes to regional specialties. It's a great spot to relax after a day of hiking.

- **Ray's Tavern:** A beloved institution in Green River, Ray's is known for its simple, delicious burgers and steaks cooked to perfection. It's a favorite among locals and those in the know for its no-frills atmosphere and friendly service.

Hanksville, Utah:

- **Duke's Slickrock Grill:** Offering hearty, campfire-style meals, Duke's has a menu that features Western favorites like ribs and grilled chicken, all served in a rustic setting that reflects the area's outdoor spirit.

- **Stan's Burger Shak:** Known for its classic burger joint menu, Stan's is the go-to place in Hanksville for a quick, satisfying meal, including shakes, burgers, and fries.

Torrey, Utah:

- **Slackers Burger Joint:** Located in Torrey, Slackers is famous for its burgers and casual, laid-back atmosphere.

It's a great local spot to refuel after exploring Capitol Reef or the surrounding areas.

- **Café Diablo:** Offers a fine dining experience with innovative Southwestern cuisine that includes unique dishes such as rattlesnake cakes. The outdoor seating area provides a pleasant atmosphere to enjoy a meal under the vast Utah sky.

Moab, Utah:

- **Milt's Stop & Eat:** Moab's oldest restaurant offers a nostalgic dining experience with burgers and shakes made from locally sourced ingredients. It's a small, retro diner with lots of local character.

- **The Spoke on Center:** Combining great food with a friendly atmosphere, The Spoke offers a menu that includes everything from gourmet burgers to vegetarian dishes, making it a perfect spot for groups with diverse tastes.

These eateries provide a taste of the local cuisine and offer a glimpse into the community's culture, making them perfect stops during your exploration of Utah's natural landscapes.

Parowan Gap

Parowan Gap is a fascinating natural landmark located in southern Utah, renowned for its unique geological formations and for its rich archaeological significance. This narrow pass through the Red Hills is home to one of the most concentrated collections of Native American petroglyphs in the region, making it a significant cultural and historical site. The Gap itself is a wind gap, an unusual geological formation where a mountain pass has been carved not by streams but by powerful winds.

Geological Features

Parowan Gap consists of a deep, narrow passage carved through the Red Hills, primarily composed of limestone and shale. These rock formations are part of the larger geological strata that stretch across the region, characterized by their distinct layers that tell a story of ancient seas and dramatic shifts in the earth's crust. The Gap is not a water-formed canyon but a wind gap, created and enlarged by the erosional force of wind over millennia. This natural corridor serves as a dramatic demonstration of wind erosion and its power to sculpt the landscape on a grand scale.

The walls of Parowan Gap are adorned with natural formations that include jagged outcrops, layered rock faces, and various erosional features that create a striking visual landscape. The area surrounding the gap also features rolling hills and isolated formations that contribute to the dramatic and rugged terrain characteristic of southern Utah.

Historical Significance

Parowan Gap is a geological wonder and a site of immense historical and cultural importance. The Gap's rock walls feature hundreds of petroglyphs carved by Native American tribes thousands of years ago.

These petroglyphs are believed to represent a variety of themes, from hunting and agriculture to astronomical symbols and mythological creatures. The site is particularly famous for its "Zipper" glyph, which is thought to be a form of a calendar or a map aligning with solar and lunar cycles.

The significance of Parowan Gap extends into the more recent past. The area was used as a passageway by early Native American tribes, and later by pioneers and settlers of European descent. The Gap has been studied extensively by archaeologists and historians aiming to understand the lives and movements of these early inhabitants and their interaction with the environment.

Off-Peak Seasons

The best time to visit Parowan Gap to avoid the crowds and fully appreciate its tranquility and historical depth is during the off-peak seasons:

- **Late Fall:** The cooler temperatures make exploring the site more comfortable, and the lower visitor numbers provide a more intimate experience with the petroglyphs.

- **Winter:** Winter visits can offer a stark beauty with occasional snow highlighting the petroglyphs and rock formations, providing excellent photographic opportunities. Visitor numbers are at their lowest during this season.

- **Early Spring:** Before the arrival of the busy tourist season, early spring can be ideal with mild weather and the chance to see the surrounding landscape begin to bloom, enhancing the natural beauty of the Gap.

Visiting during these times allows for a peaceful exploration of Parowan Gap's unique geological features and ancient petroglyphs, making for a profound and memorable experience.

Weekday vs. Weekend Visits

Choosing to visit Parowan Gap during the weekdays rather than weekends can significantly enhance the quality and enjoyment of your experience. Here are some of the benefits of scheduling a weekday visit:

- **Reduced Crowds:** Weekdays typically see fewer visitors, which means more solitude and a quieter atmosphere for contemplation and exploration of the site. This is particularly beneficial at a historical site like Parowan Gap, where the ability to quietly reflect on the ancient petroglyphs can deepen the visitor's appreciation and understanding.

- **Unhindered Access:** With fewer people around, you have better access to the most popular parts of the Gap, especially the petroglyphs. This also means less time waiting for others to move out of your desired photo shots and more unobstructed views.

- **Enhanced Interaction with Nature:** A less crowded environment enhances the chances of observing local wildlife in their natural settings. Additionally, the quiet of a weekday visit helps in absorbing the natural soundscape of the area.

- **Personal Engagement:** Fewer visitors allow for more personal interaction with any on-site guides or rangers, who can provide deeper insights into the historical and cultural significance of the petroglyphs and the natural features of the gap.

Time of Day Strategies

The time of day can greatly influence your experience at Parowan Gap, especially in terms of lighting for photography and temperature comfort. Here's how to make the most of early morning and late afternoon visits:

Early Morning Visits:

- **Advantages:** The early morning light is soft and often ideal for photographing the petroglyphs, which can appear more defined under the gentle illumination. Cooler temperatures make for a more comfortable exploration, and the quiet of the morning enhances the spiritual and historical ambiance of the site.

- **Experience:** Arrive just after sunrise to capture the best light and enjoy the peace of the site before any crowds might arrive.

Late Afternoon Visits:

- **Advantages:** The setting sun casts a golden hue over the rocks, enhancing the natural reds and oranges of the stone and highlighting the petroglyphs in a dramatic light. Temperatures begin to drop, making it more comfortable to explore.

- **Experience:** Plan to stay through sunset to experience the changing light conditions which can dramatically alter the appearance of the glyphs and the landscape.

Exploring Lesser-Known Areas

Parowan Gap is relatively compact, but the surrounding regions offer numerous opportunities to explore lesser-known areas that are equally fascinating:

Cathedral Valley:

- **Features:** Located in Capitol Reef National Park, Cathedral Valley is renowned for its monolithic sandstone formations, which are less frequented than the park's main attractions.

- **Experience:** A visit here can be combined with a trip to the Parowan Gap, offering a day-long exploration of stunning landscapes and geological features.

Waterpocket Fold:

- **Features:** Also in Capitol Reef, this area offers extended hikes and drives along less crowded trails and roads, showcasing expansive views and diverse geological formations.

- **Experience:** Explore the Fold's canyons and caprocks for a more rugged and isolated adventure, perfect for those looking to escape the more trafficked paths and dive deeper into the wild.

These strategies can help maximize your visit to Parowan Gap, ensuring you experience the site's historical richness and natural beauty under the best conditions possible.

Sample Itineraries for Crowded Days

Visiting Parowan Gap during crowded days requires strategic planning to make the most of your trip while avoiding congested areas. Here's a sample itinerary to help you navigate the site effectively:

Early Morning: Start at the Petroglyphs

- **Activity:** Begin your visit early in the morning to view the petroglyphs while the site is less crowded and the morning light provides excellent visibility and photo opportunities.

- **Highlight:** Enjoy the intricate details of the ancient carvings without the disturbance of large groups, making it easier to take unobstructed photos and contemplate the history.

Mid-Morning: Explore the Gap's Geology

- **Activity:** As the morning progresses and more visitors arrive, take a walk through the gap itself to explore its geological features. The natural wind gap formation offers impressive sights of the surrounding landscape.

- **Highlight:** The walk through the gap allows you to see and learn about the unique geological formations that characterize the area, away from the main concentration of visitors near the petroglyphs.

Lunch Break: Picnic Nearby

- **Activity:** Pack a lunch and enjoy a picnic in a less frequented area near Parowan Gap. Utilize nearby public lands or designated picnic areas for a quiet break.

- **Highlight:** A picnic provides a relaxing way to recharge before continuing your exploration, plus it keeps you onsite and ready to visit more areas in the afternoon.

Afternoon: Lesser-Known Local Sites

- **Activity:** In the afternoon, when the petroglyph area is likely at its busiest, visit other nearby attractions that are less known and frequented, such as Red Canyon or local state parks.

- **Highlight:** Exploring these alternative sites can offer more solitude and equally enriching experiences with nature and local geology.

Flexible Itinerary Ideas

Being adaptable with your plans based on real-time crowd levels can greatly enhance your experience at Parowan Gap:

High Crowd Levels:

- **Switch Times:** If you arrive to find the petroglyphs overcrowded, consider exploring the geological features first and returning to the petroglyphs later in the day when it might be quieter.

Moderate Crowd Levels:

- **Be Dynamic:** Monitor the ebb and flow of visitors and be ready to adjust your activities. For example, if a school group arrives, you might choose that moment to take your lunch break or explore an adjacent trail.

Low Crowd Levels:

- **Take Full Advantage:** With fewer visitors, take the opportunity to spend more time at each feature, dig deeper into available information, and perhaps engage more with any onsite guides or informational resources.

Off-the-Beaten-Path Hikes

For those looking to escape the crowds and explore lesser-known trails around Parowan Gap, consider these options:

Cassidy Arch Trail:

- **Location:** Situated in Capitol Reef National Park, this trail is ideal for those willing to take a short drive for a different experience. The hike leads to an impressive natural arch and offers stunning views of the park's rugged terrain.

- **Experience:** This trail sees fewer visitors compared to the main areas of Capitol Reef, providing a more secluded hiking experience.

Sulphur Creek Hike:

- **Features:** Also in Capitol Reef, this hike follows a creek through a deep canyon and involves some river walking and mild scrambling.

- **Experience:** It's a less traveled route that offers a chance to see natural pools and water-carved rock formations away from the crowds.

These itineraries and suggestions aim to optimize your visit to Parowan Gap and surrounding areas, ensuring a memorable and enjoyable experience despite the potential crowds.

Wildlife Viewing and Nature Photography

Engaging in wildlife viewing and nature photography at Parowan Gap can be a rewarding experience when done respectfully and responsibly. Here are some best practices to follow:

- **Maintain a Safe Distance:** Always keep a safe distance from wildlife to avoid causing stress or altering their behavior. Use a good quality zoom lens for photography to capture close-up images without getting too close.

- **Move Slowly and Quietly:** Be mindful of your movements and noise levels. Sudden movements or loud sounds can startle animals, leading them to flee and ruining your chance for observation or photography.

- **Use Natural Light:** Rely on natural light as much as possible for photography. Flash photography can disturb animals, particularly during twilight or nighttime, when many species are most active.

- **Stay on Designated Paths:** Keeping to established trails helps protect natural habitats and minimizes your impact on the environment, ensuring that wildlife remains undisturbed.

- **Be Patient:** Successful wildlife viewing and photography often require patience. Animals may take time to reappear after any disturbances. Spending more time quietly observing your surroundings increases your chances of a meaningful encounter.

- **Respect the Environment:** Do not attempt to feed wildlife or encroach on their habitat. Feeding animals can disrupt their natural diet and lead to unhealthy dependencies on human-provided food.

Stargazing Opportunities

Parowan Gap is renowned for its historical and geological significance and for its clear, dark skies, making it an excellent spot for stargazing. Here are some tips to enhance your stargazing experience:

- **Check the Lunar Calendar:** Plan your stargazing around the new moon phase to experience the darkest skies. Light from a full moon can wash out the stars and other celestial objects.

- **Use Red Light Flashlights:** When navigating or reading star maps during your stargazing session, use flashlights with red bulbs. Red light interferes less with night vision than white light.

- **Bring the Right Equipment:** A telescope or a pair of binoculars can significantly enhance your ability to see stars, planets, and other celestial phenomena.

- **Seek Open Spaces:** Look for open areas away from tall structures or trees to get the most expansive view of the night sky. Parowan Gap's open landscapes provide unobstructed views of the heavens.

- **Dress Appropriately:** Desert temperatures can drop significantly at night, even during summer months. Bring warm clothing and blankets to stay comfortable while you observe the night sky.

Where to Stay

When visiting Parowan Gap, choosing to stay in nearby towns can provide both convenient access to the site and a quieter, more relaxing environment away from busier tourist hubs:

- **Cedar City:** Located about 20 miles from Parowan Gap, Cedar City offers a variety of lodging options, from hotels and motels to bed and breakfasts. It's a great base for exploring the Parowan Gap and other nearby attractions.

- **Parowan:** Even closer, the small town of Parowan provides a handful of quaint accommodations, offering a more intimate setting and quick access to the Parowan Gap.

- **Brian Head:** About 30 miles from Parowan Gap, Brian Head offers a more resort-like atmosphere, hotel and condo rentals, and access to recreational activities.

- **Torrey:** Although further away, staying in Torrey is an excellent option for those also planning to visit Capitol Reef National Park. It offers a range of accommodations, including hotels, inns, and guesthouses.

These locations provide varied lodging options, catering to different preferences and allowing visitors to choose accommodations that best suit their travel style while exploring Parowan Gap and the surrounding areas.

Dining Recommendations

When visiting Parowan Gap and the surrounding areas, indulging in local cuisine at lesser-known eateries can provide a more authentic and intimate dining experience. Here are some highly recommended spots in nearby towns that are favored by locals and offer excellent food away from the main tourist routes:

Parowan:

- **Hometown Cafe:** Known for its home-style cooking and friendly atmosphere, Hometown Cafe is a favorite among locals. Try their breakfast menu, which includes everything from hearty omelets to homemade biscuits and gravy.

- **Parowan Café:** A small-town diner that offers a variety of classic American dishes. The café is particularly famous for its pies, which are all baked fresh daily.

Cedar City:

- **Centro Woodfired Pizzeria:** Located in the heart of Cedar City, this pizzeria is well-loved for its artisan pizzas made with locally sourced ingredients and cooked in a traditional wood-fired oven. The vibrant atmosphere and excellent service make it a top choice for dinner.

- **The French Spot:** Offering authentic French cuisine, The French Spot is run by a French chef who brings the flavors of France to Utah. The menu features specialties like quiche, savory crepes, and freshly baked pastries.

Brian Head:

- **Pizanos Pizzeria:** In the resort town of Brian Head, Pizanos offers delicious pizza in a cozy setting. It's a great spot to relax after a day of outdoor activities, and they also offer a selection of local beers.

- **The Last Chair Saloon:** Located at Brian Head Resort, this saloon offers a warm, rustic atmosphere with a menu that includes comfort food favorites such as burgers, chili, and hearty stews.

Beaver:

- **Crazy Cow Café:** Just a short drive from Parowan, the Crazy Cow Café in Beaver is known for its friendly service and an extensive menu that includes everything from pancakes to steak dinners. The restaurant prides itself on its "home cooking" vibe.

- **Timberline Inn Restaurant:** For those looking for a more upscale dining experience, the Timberline Inn offers a fine dining atmosphere with a menu that features prime rib, fresh trout, and a variety of pasta dishes.

These eateries offer delicious food and contribute to a genuine local experience, allowing visitors to enjoy the regional flavors and warm hospitality of southern Utah.

Coral Pink Sand Dunes State Park

Coral Pink Sand Dunes State Park, located in southwestern Utah near Kanab, offers a stunning panorama of shifting pink dunes framed by red sandstone cliffs and deep blue skies. This state park covers approximately 3,730 acres and is renowned for its vibrant pink-hued sand dunes, which owe their unique color to the iron oxide (rust) staining the sand. Formed from the erosion of pink Navajo Sandstone surrounding the park, these dunes are an ever-changing landscape shaped by the winds that frequently sweep through the Paria Valley.

Geological Features

Coral Pink Sand Dunes State Park is characterized by its large, undulating dunes of warm, pink sand, which are the main attraction and a rare sight in the American Southwest. These dunes are dynamic, formed by the erosion of the surrounding sandstone cliffs and constantly reshaped by the wind. This geological process creates a variety of dune types within the park, including parabolic and transverse dunes, each offering different textures and patterns for exploration and photography.

The dunes are estimated to be between 10,000 and 15,000 years old, and their formation continues today as wind patterns deposit new layers of sand. The park's dunes can reach heights of up to 100 feet, providing dramatic views and a surreal desert landscape that contrasts sharply with the green juniper and pinion pines that dot the edges of the dune field.

Historical Significance

Coral Pink Sand Dunes has served as both a natural barrier and a passageway for various groups over the centuries, from early Native American tribes to European settlers. The area was traditionally used by the Navajo and Paiute tribes for hunting and gathering, utilizing the unique flora and fauna of the region. In the 19th and early 20th centuries, Mormon pioneers moved through the area, and the dunes served as a landmark on their trek across the desert.

The park's establishment as a state park in 1963 aimed to preserve its unique geological features while allowing the public to enjoy and learn about this dynamic landscape. Today, it serves as an important recreational and educational resource, illustrating the natural processes of wind-driven dune formation.

Off-Peak Seasons

The best times to visit Coral Pink Sand Dunes State Park to avoid crowds and experience the area in relative solitude are during the off-peak seasons:

- **Late Fall:** The temperatures cool down, making hiking and exploration of the dunes more comfortable. The lower angle of the sun enriches the color of the sand, enhancing photographic opportunities.

- **Winter:** Snow occasionally dusts the dunes, creating a stunning contrast of pink sand and white snow. Winter is the least crowded season, offering a unique and quiet landscape.

- **Early Spring:** Before the busy summer months arrive, the weather in early spring is ideal for visiting the park. Wildflowers begin to bloom around the dunes, adding splashes of color to the sandy landscape.

Visiting during these times ensures a more tranquil experience, allowing visitors to fully appreciate the natural beauty and serenity of Coral Pink Sand Dunes State Park.

Weekday vs. Weekend Visits

Visiting Coral Pink Sand Dunes State Park on weekdays rather than weekends can profoundly enhance your experience due to significantly reduced crowds. Here are some key benefits of choosing a weekday visit:

- **Enhanced Solitude:** Weekdays generally see fewer visitors, allowing for a more peaceful and intimate interaction with the natural environment. The tranquility enhances the sensory experience, making the sound of the wind and the sight of shifting sands more profound.

- **Unobstructed Access:** With fewer people around, you have better access to popular spots within the park without the need to navigate through crowds. This means more freedom to explore at your own pace and the ability to take unimpeded photographs of the stunning dune landscape.

- **Increased Wildlife Sightings:** The reduced human presence during weekdays increases the likelihood of encountering wildlife. Typically shy animals might be more visible and active, providing excellent opportunities for wildlife photography.

- **Personal Engagement:** Fewer visitors allow for more personal interactions with park staff, who can offer detailed insights into the park's ecology, geology, and history without the distractions of larger crowds.

Time of Day Strategies

The time of day you choose to visit Coral Pink Sand Dunes can significantly affect your experience, especially in terms of lighting for photography and temperature comfort. Here's how to optimize early morning and late afternoon visits:

Early Morning Visits:

- **Advantages:** The early morning light is particularly magical at the dunes, enhancing the pink and red hues of the sand. Cooler temperatures make hiking and climbing the dunes more comfortable.

- **Experience:** Morning is an ideal time for photography as the low angle of the sun creates dramatic shadows that define the shapes and textures of the dunes. It's also a peaceful time to enjoy the serenity of the landscape.

Late Afternoon Visits:

- **Advantages:** Late afternoon and sunset bring a golden glow to the sand, transforming the landscape into a warm, radiant scene. Temperatures begin to cool, making the sand more comfortable to walk on.

- **Experience:** This time is perfect for capturing the changing colors of the sky as the sun sets. The dunes become less crowded, offering a more secluded experience to watch the sunset.

Exploring Lesser-Known Areas

While the main dune field is the primary attraction, Coral Pink Sand Dunes State Park also offers access to lesser-known areas that are equally captivating and usually less crowded:

Cathedral Valley:

- Located in Capitol Reef National Park, Cathedral Valley is an excellent side trip for those staying near Coral Pink Sand Dunes. Known for its monolithic sandstone formations, this remote area offers solitude and stunning desert landscapes.

Waterpocket Fold:

- Also, in Capitol Reef, the Waterpocket Fold extends much further and offers a range of hiking and exploring opportunities away from popular spots. It features striking geological formations and provides a sense of vast wilderness.

These areas provide excellent alternatives for visitors looking to escape the more frequented paths and explore the diverse landscapes the region has to offer. Each location offers unique geological features and a quieter setting for hiking, photography, and nature observation.

Sample Itineraries for Crowded Days

When visiting Coral Pink Sand Dunes State Park on crowded days, it's crucial to plan your activities to circumvent the busiest areas and times. Here's a sample itinerary to help you make the most of your visit:

Early Morning: Dune Exploration

- **Activity:** Start your day early by exploring the main dune field. Early mornings provide cooler temperatures and optimal lighting for photography and have fewer visitors.

- **Highlight:** Use this time to hike to the highest dunes for panoramic views of the park. The morning light casts dramatic shadows on the dunes, perfect for photography.

Mid-Morning: Visitor Center and Exhibits

- **Activity:** As the crowds begin to fill the dunes, head to the visitor center. Use this opportunity to learn about the park's natural history, geology, and the formation of the dunes through interactive exhibits.

- **Highlight:** Engaging with the educational content can enhance your understanding of the dune ecosystem, enriching your experience of the park.

Lunch: Picnic at Designated Area

- **Activity:** Enjoy a packed lunch at one of the park's picnic areas. This is a good time to rest and plan your afternoon activities.

- **Highlight:** Picnic areas usually offer shade and facilities, providing a comfortable break from the desert sun.

Afternoon: Nature Trails

- **Activity:** Post lunch, explore the lesser-visited nature trails that offer diverse landscapes and quieter hiking options. Trails like the Coral Pink Sand Dunes Nature Trail offer a short, scenic loop that is generally less crowded.

- **Highlight:** These trails provide opportunities to see wildlife and native vegetation, offering a different perspective of the park's ecosystem.

Flexible Itinerary Ideas

Flexibility can greatly enhance your experience, especially on crowded days. Here are some strategies based on varying crowd levels:

High Crowd Levels:

- **Switch Activities:** If the dunes are overly crowded, consider visiting local attractions outside the park, such as nearby hiking areas or historic sites. Return to the dunes later in the afternoon when the crowds may have thinned.

Moderate Crowd Levels:

- **Dynamic Adjustments:** Monitor different areas of the park. If your planned destination is busy, have backup options ready, such as less popular viewing spots or trails.

Low Crowd Levels:

- **Take Advantage:** If the park is less crowded than expected, explore more extensively. Visit popular spots or engage in activities like sand sledding or photography that benefit from having fewer people around.

Off-the-Beaten-Path Hikes

Exploring lesser-known trails can provide a peaceful alternative to the main attractions:

Cassidy Arch Trail:

- **Location:** Capitol Reef National Park, about a two-hour drive from Coral Pink Sand Dunes.

- **Experience:** This trail is less trafficked compared to the park's main routes and offers a stunning arch formation as the payoff, along with impressive canyon views.

South Fork Indian Canyon:

- **Features:** Located near the park, this area offers secluded hikes, ancient rock art, and dramatic cliff views.

- **Experience:** The trails are usually quiet and provide a more immersive experience of the local culture and natural beauty.

These itineraries and hiking suggestions are designed to optimize your visit to Coral Pink Sand Dunes State Park. They allow for both planned and spontaneous exploration based on real-time conditions and crowd levels.

Wildlife Viewing and Nature Photography

Wildlife viewing and photography at Coral Pink Sand Dunes State Park can be enriching activities if conducted with respect for the natural environment and its inhabitants. Here are some best practices to follow:

- **Maintain Distance:** Always keep a safe distance from wildlife to avoid disturbing them. Use binoculars and telephoto lenses to observe or photograph animals without getting too close.

- **Move slowly and Quietly:** To avoid startling wildlife, move slowly and keep noise levels low. This approach helps you observe natural behaviors and enhances your chances of seeing more elusive species.

- **Use Natural Lighting:** Rely on natural light as much as possible for photography. Avoid using flash, which can disturb animals, especially during dawn and dusk, when many animals are most active.

- **Stay on Trails:** Keep to designated paths to minimize impact on the park's ecosystem. This helps protect animal habitats and reduces the likelihood of disturbing wildlife.

- **Be Patient:** Good wildlife viewing and photography require patience. Wait calmly and quietly for wildlife to appear. Often, animals that have initially been disturbed will return once they feel safe.

- **Respect the Environment:** Do not feed wildlife or attempt to attract their attention for photos. Feeding wildlife can alter natural behaviors and potentially cause harm.

Stargazing Opportunities

Coral Pink Sand Dunes State Park, with its remote location and minimal light pollution, offers excellent stargazing opportunities. Here are some tips for a rewarding night sky experience:

- **Check Moon Phases:** Plan your stargazing around the new moon when the sky is darkest. Light from a full moon can obscure dimmer stars.

- **Use Red Light Flashlights:** Use red light flashlights when navigating or setting up equipment in the dark to preserve your night vision and minimize light pollution.

- **Bring Proper Gear:** A telescope or a pair of binoculars can enhance your viewing experience, allowing you to see more than with the naked eye. A star map or a stargazing app can also help identify constellations and celestial bodies.

- **Choose Open Areas:** Open areas away from the dunes and vegetation offer the best-unobstructed views of the sky. The park's main dune field can provide a dramatic foreground for night photography.

- **Dress Appropriately:** Nights in the desert can be cold, even in summer. Dress in layers and bring extra blankets or a chair for comfort during extended viewing periods.

Where to Stay

When visiting Coral Pink Sand Dunes State Park, staying in nearby towns can enhance your experience by offering comfortable lodging away from the crowds:

- **Kanab:** Located about 30 minutes from the park, Kanab offers a range of lodging options, from hotels and motels to charming bed and breakfasts. It's a great base for exploring the wider region, including other nearby national parks.

- **Mount Carmel Junction:** Just 20 minutes from the park, this area offers some smaller motels and inns, providing easy access to the park and a quiet, rural setting.

- **Page, Arizona:** Although about a 90-minute drive from the park, Page provides a variety of accommodations and is an excellent option if you plan to visit other attractions, such as Lake Powell or Antelope Canyon.

- **Torrey:** For those visiting multiple parks, Torrey is about two hours away but offers access to both Capitol Reef National Park and Coral Pink Sand Dunes. Torrey has several hotels, guesthouses, and camping options.

These locations provide diverse accommodations to suit various preferences and budgets, making your visit to Coral Pink Sand Dunes State Park both enjoyable and convenient.

Dining Recommendations

When visiting Coral Pink Sand Dunes State Park, exploring local dining options that are less frequented by tourists can offer a more authentic and relaxing culinary experience. Here are some recommended eateries in nearby towns that provide delicious meals favored by locals:

Kanab, Utah:

- **Peekaboo Canyon Wood Fired Kitchen:** Known for its creative vegetarian and vegan dishes, this restaurant offers a cozy atmosphere, wood-fired pizzas, and fresh, locally sourced ingredients. It's a great spot for those looking for healthy, flavorful options.

- **Rocking V Cafe:** This cafe offers a mix of American and Southwestern dishes with a focus on quality and creativity. It is popular among locals for its art-filled interiors and friendly service, making it a must-visit for a unique dining experience.

- **Houston's Trail's End Restaurant:** For those craving traditional comfort food, Houston's serves up hearty meals in a casual setting. It's well-loved for breakfasts that offer a robust start to a day of adventure.

Page, Arizona:

- **BirdHouse:** A relatively new yet quickly beloved spot, BirdHouse serves up delicious fried chicken and sides in a casual and friendly environment. Their meals are perfect for a comfort food fix after a day of exploring.

- **Big John's Texas BBQ:** Offering a laid-back outdoor setting, Big John's provides authentic Texas barbecue. It's a favorite for both locals and savvy visitors looking for genuine smoked meats and a great atmosphere.

Fredonia, Arizona:

- **Juniper Ridge Restaurant:** This family-owned restaurant offers American cuisine with a home-cooked feel. Known for its welcoming staff and good portions, Juniper Ridge is ideal for travelers looking for a warm meal in a homey setting.

Mount Carmel Junction, Utah:

- **Thunderbird Restaurant:** Famous for its motto "Home of the Ho-Made Pies," the Thunderbird Restaurant offers comforting diner classics, including some of the best pies in the area. It's a great stop for a casual meal in a nostalgic setting.

These dining options cater to a variety of tastes and contribute to a genuine local experience, allowing you to enjoy regional flavors and warm hospitality while visiting Coral Pink Sand Dunes State Park and its surroundings.

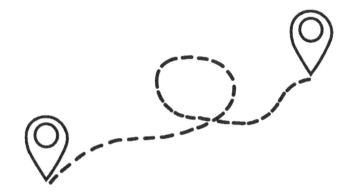

CHAPTER 3

Crowded Destinations for Crowd Haters

Southern Utah, a land where the earth opens up to reveal its soul, is a paradox for the introverted traveler. Here, the monumental splendors of Zion, Bryce Canyon, Moab, and Arches beckon with their otherworldly landscapes, promising solitude in their vastness—yet often delivering crowds that swarm like ants across sugar. It's an intriguing conundrum: these parks offer experiences that are both quintessentially solitary and unavoidably communal.

Why Visit Zion, Bryce Canyon, Moab, and Arches Despite the Crowds?

At first blush, the introvert's heart might quail at the thought of navigating throngs of tourists, each armed with cameras and wide-eyed enthusiasm. However, there are compelling reasons to brave these populated portals to nature's majesty:

- **Unmatched Natural Beauty:** Each of these parks houses unique geological wonders that are not just photographs but experiences. Zion's towering cliffs of Navajo sandstone, Bryce Canyon's haunting hoodoos, the surreal landscape of Arches, and Moab's red rock vistas offer a visual feast that transcends the annoyance of crowds.

- **Transformational Experiences:** These landscapes wield the power to transform. They remind us of our smallness, not just in stature but in tenure. They have stood the test of eons, their beauty sculpted by the slow, relentless artistry of nature. Such experiences can be grounding and profoundly moving, offering moments of introspection and connection to the earth that are rare in our daily lives.

- **Well-Managed Visitor Programs:** Despite their popularity, these parks are managed with an eye toward preserving both the visitor experience and the natural environment. Shuttle systems in Zion, designated viewpoints in Bryce, timed entries in Arches, and expansive recreational areas around Moab help distribute tourists in ways that can minimize human impact and maximize individual enjoyment.

- **Seasonal and Time-of-Day Strategies:** For those willing to venture beyond the comfort of temperate weather and convenient hours, visiting these parks during off-peak seasons or times of day can offer a more secluded experience. Early mornings and late afternoons, as well as colder months, see fewer visitors, allowing for quieter exploration.

- **Paths Less Traveled:** Each park has its well-trodden paths and overlooks, but also lesser-known trails and hidden corners where one can escape the crowds. Finding these spots often requires research or the assistance of park rangers, but the reward is a more personal encounter with these stunning landscapes.

The call of Southern Utah's iconic parks is not to be ignored lightly, even by those of us who treasure solitude. With thoughtful planning, an understanding of each park's layout and visitor management strategies, and a willingness to embrace the early hours or colder seasons, even the most crowd-averse can find quiet moments of awe and beauty. After all, sometimes, the path to solitude is taken by walking straight through the crowd.

Zion National Park

Zion National Park, a jewel of the American Southwest, is nestled in the heart of southern Utah. Known for its dramatic landscapes and towering cliffs, Zion draws millions of visitors each year, captivated by its raw beauty and majestic vistas. The park covers 229 square miles of high plateaus, rock towers, and deep, narrow canyons, showcasing a diverse range of ecosystems and topographies.

Geological Features

The geological story of Zion National Park is one of immense natural architecture, sculpted by the forces of erosion over millions of years. The most prominent feature of the park is its vast collection of sandstone cliffs, ranging in color from cream to deep red. These cliffs are primarily composed of Navajo sandstone, which has been eroded by the Virgin River into a myriad of shapes, including plateaus, towers, mesas, and slot canyons.

Zion is renowned for its impressive rock formations, such as the iconic Angels Landing and the Great White Throne. The park's unique geology is a spectacle of natural beauty and provides insight into the Earth's evolutionary history. Over time, the relentless force of water has carved deep into the desert floor, creating the Zion Canyon, which is up to half a mile deep in places.

The park's landscape is a dynamic display of nature's power, where visitors can observe steep cliffs, canyons, rock towers, and high mesas. Additionally, the Kolob Canyons in the northwest part of the park offer a more secluded experience with their own unique geological features, including crimson canyons and towering cliffs.

Historical Significance

Zion National Park is rich in cultural history, having been home to various indigenous groups for thousands of years. The Ancestral Puebloans and later the Paiute tribes inhabited the region, leaving behind a legacy of rock art, artifacts, and storied places that speak to their deep connection with the landscape.

In the early 20th century, Mormon pioneers settled in the area, drawn by the land's stark beauty and the promise of solitude and spiritual sustenance. The park was originally named Mukuntuweap National Monument by the U.S. government in 1909 but was later renamed Zion, a term used by the Mormons to denote a place of peace and refuge.

Off-Peak Seasons

Visiting Zion National Park during the off-peak seasons can significantly enhance the experience, allowing for quieter exploration and personal reflection:

- **Late Fall:** The temperatures cool down, and the summer crowds have dissipated, making it an ideal time for hiking and photography. The fall colors against the backdrop of Zion's cliffs offer a spectacular display.

- **Winter:** Zion in winter is a quiet wonderland, with occasional snowfalls that dust the red rocks in white. Fewer visitors during this season means more solitude and a unique view of the park's features.

- **Early Spring:** Before the rush of the peak tourist season, early spring brings mild weather and a rejuvenated landscape, with wildflowers beginning to bloom and waterfalls fed by snowmelt at their fullest.

Visiting during these times offers a more tranquil experience, allowing visitors to appreciate the park's natural beauty without the crowds.

Weekday vs. Weekend Visits

Opting for a weekday visit to Zion National Park can significantly enhance the quality of your experience, thanks to a reduction in crowd sizes and a more relaxed atmosphere. Here are some key benefits:

- **Decreased Crowds:** On weekdays, Zion National Park is considerably less crowded than on weekends. This reduction in visitor numbers means shorter lines at shuttle stops, less traffic on the scenic drives, and more solitude on the trails, which can greatly enhance your connection with nature.

- **Enhanced Wildlife Viewing:** With fewer people around, wildlife is more likely to be visible. Weekdays provide a better opportunity to encounter Zion's diverse wildlife, such as mule deer, bighorn sheep, and various bird species, as they are less disturbed by human presence.

- **Easier Access to Popular Sites:** Iconic spots like Angels Landing and The Narrows are less congested on weekdays. This allows for a more enjoyable and safer hiking experience, where you can take your time to enjoy the views and take photographs without feeling rushed.

- **More Personal Space:** The serene environment on weekdays offers a more personal experience, allowing you to appreciate the majestic beauty of the park's cliffs, canyons, and vistas without the noise and interruptions often found on busier days.

Time of Day Strategies

Choosing the right time of day for your visit can greatly influence your experience at Zion National Park, especially when it comes to avoiding crowds and experiencing the park's natural beauty in the best possible light.

Early Morning Visits:

- **Advantages:** The early morning light is ideal for photography, highlighting the vibrant colors of the sandstone cliffs, and for cooler hiking temperatures. Starting your hikes early can help you avoid the midday heat and crowds, especially during the summer months.

- **Experience:** Morning is the best time to tackle challenging trails like Angels Landing or Observation Point, as the temperatures are cooler and the paths less crowded.

Late Afternoon Visits:

- **Advantages:** Late afternoon into sunset transforms the park's landscape with a golden glow, making it a prime time for photography. As many visitors start to leave, the trails and viewpoints become less crowded.

- **Experience:** Enjoying a sunset at key overlooks such as Canyon Overlook or watching the changing colors from the Human History Museum can be particularly memorable.

Popular Attractions

Zion National Park is home to some of the most iconic and frequently visited attractions in the United States. Highlighting these popular spots:

- **Angels Landing:** Known for its breathtaking views and thrilling hikes, Angels Landing attracts adventurers willing to navigate a steep, narrow ridge to the summit. The trail offers panoramic views of Zion Canyon and is a must-do for many visitors.

- **The Narrows:** Hiking The Narrows, where you wade through the Virgin River with towering canyon walls on either side, is an unforgettable experience that showcases the unique geology of Zion. It's one of the park's most distinctive and beloved adventures.

- **Emerald Pools:** This trail features a series of pools and waterfalls set against lush vegetation and dramatic cliffs. It's perfect for families and those looking for a less strenuous hike.

- **Weeping Rock:** This short, accessible trail leads to a rock alcove with dripping springs, creating a cool, mossy haven during hot summer days.

Visiting these attractions, especially with strategic timing and on less crowded days, can significantly enhance your enjoyment and appreciation of Zion National Park.

Exploring Lesser-Known Areas

Zion National Park's vastness means that beyond the crowded vistas and well-trodden paths lie lesser-known areas teeming with natural beauty but receiving far fewer visitors. Exploring these areas can offer a tranquil alternative to the park's more famous sites:

Kolob Terrace:

A high, forested plateau provides access to diverse landscapes, from high mountain meadows to dense aspen forests. The West

Rim Trail, starting from Lava Point, is less frequented and offers stunning views of the lower Zion Canyon and its rock formations.

Kolob Canyons:

Located in the northwest corner of the park, this area is accessed via a separate entrance and is often overlooked by visitors focused on Zion Canyon. The Kolob Canyons Road leads to several breathtaking viewpoints and trails, including the Timber Creek Overlook and the Taylor Creek Trail, which features two historic homesteads and a double arch alcove.

Hop Valley Trail:

For those seeking solitude, the Hop Valley Trail traverses through a serene valley with lush meadows and a stream, framed by towering sandstone cliffs. This trail is particularly appealing for its contrast to the arid, open vistas found elsewhere in the park.

Sample Itineraries for Crowded Days

When Zion National Park feels overwhelmed by visitors, having a structured plan can help you enjoy your visit without the stress of navigating through dense crowds:

Early Morning Start:

Begin your day with a sunrise hike on the Watchman Trail, less crowded than the more famous hikes and offering spectacular views of the Watchman Spire against the morning sky.

Mid-Morning Exploration:

As the main valley begins to fill, head to the Kolob Terrace section of the park. Here, you can enjoy a peaceful hike on the Middle Fork of Taylor Creek, leading to the Double Arch Alcove.

Lunch Break:

Pack a lunch to enjoy at one of the less crowded picnic areas in Kolob Canyons or along the Kolob Terrace Road, where you can relax and rejuvenate away from the bustling park center.

Late Afternoon Leisure:

In the afternoon, explore the Pa'rus Trail, a paved path along the Virgin River that is perfect for a leisurely walk or bike ride as the day cools down.

Flexible Itinerary Ideas

Having a flexible approach can greatly enhance your experience at Zion, particularly on crowded days. Here are some strategies:

Dynamic Planning:

Keep an eye on the shuttle bus lines and trailhead activity. If a popular area looks overcrowded, be prepared to switch to a secondary option quickly.

Alternative Experiences:

Consider other activities, such as attending a ranger-led program or exploring the Zion Human History Museum during peak hours when trails are busiest.

Evening Flexibility:

Take advantage of the late hours at the park, especially during the summer when daylight extends well into the evening. Trails like the Riverside Walk are magical at dusk and generally less crowded.

By integrating these lesser-known areas and flexible strategies into your visit, you can explore Zion National Park in a way that minimizes stress and maximizes your interaction with this incredible landscape, even during peak tourist seasons.

Off-the-Beaten-Path Hikes

Zion National Park offers several lesser-known trails that provide stunning natural beauty without the crowds of the park's more popular hikes. These hidden gems offer tranquility and unique landscapes:

Cassidy Arch Trail (Capitol Reef National Park):

While not in Zion itself, the Cassidy Arch Trail in nearby Capitol Reef is a spectacular hike that deserves mention. This moderately strenuous trail leads to a breathtaking natural arch named after the infamous outlaw Butch Cassidy. The arch offers a perfect frame for the expansive views of Capitol Reef's rugged terrain.

Kolob Arch via La Verkin Creek Trail:

Located in the less-visited Kolob Canyons section of Zion, this trail offers a chance to see one of the world's largest freestanding arches. The hike is challenging but rewards hikers with spectacular views of the canyon and the massive Kolob Arch.

Many Pools Trail:

This trail is an off-the-beaten-path favorite that showcases several natural pools formed by erosion. It's less marked and less maintained, offering a more adventurous route than the main park trails. Springtime visits are especially rewarding when the pools are filled with water and the surrounding desert blooms.

Chinle Trail:

For those seeking solitude, the Chinle Trail provides a long, relatively flat hike through the park's desert scrub and pinyon-juniper woodlands. This trail offers expansive views of the park's lower elevations and is particularly good for winter hikes, as it receives little to no snow.

Wildlife Viewing and Nature Photography

Zion National Park is rich in biodiversity, providing ample opportunities for wildlife viewing and nature photography. To ensure a respectful and safe experience for both wildlife and humans, consider the following practices:

Keep a Respectful Distance:

Always maintain a safe distance from animals to avoid distressing them. Use zoom lenses for photography to capture detailed images without approaching too closely.

Stay Quiet and Move Slowly:

To avoid startling wildlife, keep noise levels low and movements smooth and slow. These practices respect the animals' natural behavior and enhance your chances of observing them in their natural habitats.

Use Natural Light:

Use natural light for photography, avoiding flash, which can disrupt animal behavior, especially at dawn and dusk, when many animals are most active.

Follow Park Guidelines:

Heed all park rules regarding wildlife interaction. Feeding or attempting to attract wildlife with calls or gestures is prohibited and can be harmful.

Be Patient:

Good wildlife viewing and nature photography often require patience. Spend time quietly waiting, and nature will reveal its wonders to you.

Stargazing Opportunities

Zion National Park's remote location and dark skies make it an excellent spot for stargazing. Here are some tips to enhance your night sky viewing:

Check the Lunar Calendar:

Plan your stargazing sessions around the new moon when the sky is darkest. Avoid full moon nights, as the moonlight can wash out dimmer stars.

Seek Out Dark Areas:

For the best stargazing experiences, head to areas away from the light pollution of the park's visitor centers and campgrounds. The Kolob Canyons and remote sections of the park are ideal.

Use Proper Gear:

A telescope or a pair of good binoculars will enhance your viewing of celestial objects. A star map or a stargazing app can help you identify constellations and planets.

Dress Appropriately:

Nights in the desert can be cold, even in summer. Dress in layers and bring blankets or a comfortable chair to enjoy extended viewing.

These activities and best practices allow you to explore Zion National Park's lesser-known aspects and natural phenomena, enriching your experience while maintaining respect for the park's environment and its inhabitants.

Where to Stay

Exploring Zion National Park is an unforgettable experience, but finding a peaceful place to stay away from the crowds can enhance your visit significantly. Here are several options for lodging in nearby towns that provide both convenience and a respite from the park's busier areas:

Springdale:

Located just outside the park's main entrance, Springdale offers a variety of lodging options, from luxury resorts to quaint bed and breakfasts. While it is the closest town to the park, a careful selection of accommodations on the outskirts can offer a quieter stay.

- **Desert Pearl Inn:** Known for its beautiful riverfront views and spacious rooms, it provides a serene setting to relax after a day of hiking.

- **Canyon Vista Lodge:** Offers a more intimate experience with personalized service, set away from the main road.

Hurricane:

About a 30-minute drive from Zion, Hurricane is an excellent option for visitors looking for more economical lodging options in a less tourist-centric town.

- **Zion Gate RV Resort:** Perfect for those who prefer a home-away-from-home experience, offering spacious sites for RVs and excellent facilities.

- **Econo Lodge:** A budget-friendly hotel that provides comfortable accommodations without the frills, ideal for the cost-conscious traveler.

La Verkin:

La Verkin provides a small-town atmosphere with easy access to Zion National Park, just 20 minutes away. It's an excellent base for visitors looking to explore Zion and other nearby attractions.

- **La Verkin Creek Inn:** Known for its hospitable service and comfortable rooms, it's a great choice for those seeking a quiet retreat.

Kanab:

Located about an hour's drive from Zion, Kanab is ideal for visitors planning to explore a broader area, including Bryce Canyon National Park and the North Rim of the Grand Canyon.

- **Canyons Boutique Hotel:** A charming and elegantly furnished hotel that serves as a comfortable oasis after a long day of adventure.

Dining Recommendations

Enjoying local cuisine can be a highlight of any trip to Zion National Park. Here are some dining options in nearby towns that are favored by locals and offer authentic, less touristy experiences:

Springdale:

- **Oscar's Cafe:** Famous for its enormous portions and friendly service, Oscar's serves up delicious Mexican and American southwest dishes in a casual, lively setting.

- **Bit & Spur Restaurant & Saloon:** Offers a creative menu with Mexican-inspired flavors and a great selection of local microbrews in a rustic atmosphere.

Hurricane:

- **Main Street Cafe:** A local favorite known for its home-style cooking and warm, welcoming service, serving classic American breakfast and lunch.

- **Barista's Restaurant:** Famous for their hearty meals and homemade desserts, a must-visit for those seeking a taste of local cuisine.

La Verkin:

- **River Rock Roasting Company:** Perched on a cliff overlooking the Virgin River, this cafe offers freshly roasted coffee, great pizzas, and sandwiches, along with stunning views.

Kanab:

- **Peekaboo Canyon Wood Fired Kitchen:** Specializing in vegetarian and vegan options, this restaurant is popular for its wood-fired pizzas and fresh salads, located in a vibrant, artsy setting.

- **Houston's Trail's End Restaurant:** Known for its hearty, traditional Western meals and friendly atmosphere, it's a perfect spot to experience local hospitality and cuisine.

These accommodations and dining options provide excellent ways to enjoy the local flavor and culture while visiting Zion National Park, ensuring a restful and more authentic travel experience.

Bryce Canyon National Park

Bryce Canyon National Park, famed for its stunning crimson-colored hoodoos, stands as a grand testament to the power of natural erosion. Nestled in southern Utah, this park is less of a canyon and more of a series of giant natural amphitheaters along the eastern side of the Paunsaugunt Plateau. Renowned for its striking geological structures, Bryce offers a surreal landscape that feels almost otherworldly, drawing visitors from around the globe to witness its extraordinary formations.

Geological Features

Bryce Canyon's landscape is primarily shaped by the freeze-thaw cycle, which erodes the softer limestone that forms the hoodoos. These unique geological formations are spire-shaped rock columns that rise majestically from the canyon floor, creating a maze of stunning rock formations that vary in size from that of an average human to heights exceeding a 10-story building. The most enchanting times to view these magnificent structures are during sunrise and sunset when the light casts vibrant hues of red, orange, and white across the amphitheaters, highlighting their intricate shapes and the natural amphitheater's immense depth.

The park is home to three main amphitheaters—Bryce, Sunset, and Inspiration Point—each offering distinct views and geological features. The Navajo Loop and Queen's Garden trails provide up-close encounters with famous structures such as Thor's Hammer and Wall Street, a narrow switchback trail weaving between towering rocks. The geological history of Bryce Canyon involves sediment deposits from ancient lakes, which solidified over millions of years into limestone, and then sculpted by nature's elements into the park's iconic hoodoos.

Historical Significance

The human history of Bryce Canyon dates back over 10,000 years, with Native American peoples such as the Paiute Indians, inhabiting the region long before European settlers. The Paiutes developed a rich mythology around the hoodoos, often describing them as "Ancient Legend People" turned to stone by Coyote, the trickster god. This mythology highlights the deep spiritual connection and respect the native peoples had for the landscape.

European Americans discovered Bryce Canyon in the 1850s when Mormon pioneers settled in the area. Ebenezer Bryce, for whom the park is named, homesteaded here in the 1870s. Bryce famously described the canyon as "a hell of a place to lose a cow," highlighting the difficult terrain. The designation of the area as a national park in 1928 was part of a broader movement to preserve and recognize the unique natural beauty of the American West for future generations.

Off-Peak Seasons

To truly appreciate the quiet magnificence of Bryce Canyon without the crowds, consider visiting during the off-peak seasons:

- **Late Fall:** The cooler temperatures and fewer tourists make late fall an ideal time to explore the park. The air is crisp, and the low-hanging sun casts long shadows, enriching the colors of the hoodoos.

- **Winter:** Winter transforms the park into a tranquil, snowy wonderland. Snow-dusted hoodoos offer a stark contrast to the bright red rocks, providing spectacular photo opportunities. Fewer visitors and serene snow-covered landscapes make winter an exceptional time for a peaceful visit.

- **Early Spring:** Before the spring break crowds arrive, early spring in Bryce Canyon is refreshingly brisk. Melting snow feeds into natural creeks, and wildlife returns throughout the park. This season allows visitors to enjoy the rebirth of the park's flora and fauna.

Visiting Bryce Canyon during these times means fewer human encounters and personal communion with nature's quiet beauty, making for a truly memorable experience.

Weekday vs. Weekend Visits

Visiting Bryce Canyon National Park on weekdays as opposed to weekends offers several advantages that can significantly enhance the visitor experience. Opting for a weekday excursion allows for a more intimate connection with the stunning natural environment, free from the bustling crowds typical of weekend visits.

- **Reduced Crowds:** The most apparent benefit of weekday visits is the smaller number of visitors. This reduction in crowd size means shorter lines at the visitor center, less crowded viewpoints and trails, and more opportunities to enjoy the park's tranquility.

- **Enhanced Wildlife Viewing:** With fewer people around, wildlife is more likely to appear near trails and within the park's boundaries. This makes weekdays ideal for wildlife enthusiasts and photographers aiming to capture natural behavior without human interference.

- **Greater Accessibility:** Parking at popular trailheads and overlooks is more accessible during weekdays. This convenience can make a significant difference, especially during peak tourist seasons when finding parking on weekends can be challenging.

- **More Enjoyable Hiking Experience:** Trails are less congested on weekdays, which makes hiking safer and more enjoyable. Visitors can take their time, stopping to enjoy the panoramic views and unique geological formations without feeling rushed or crowded.

Time of Day Strategies

Choosing the right time of day to visit popular trails in Bryce Canyon can greatly affect your experience. The park's high elevation and exposed trails mean that weather conditions can change quickly, and the sun can be intense.

Early Morning Visits:

- **Advantages:** The early morning light enhances the red and orange hues of the hoodoos and makes for cooler temperatures. Starting your hike early can help you avoid the midday sun and heat, particularly during the summer months.

- **Experience:** Morning is the ideal time to photograph Bryce Canyon's famous hoodoos as the light enhances their colors and casts dramatic shadows. Trails like the Navajo Loop and Fairyland Loop are particularly stunning in the early morning light.

Late Afternoon Visits:

- **Advantages:** Late afternoon brings softer light and cooler temperatures, making it a perfect time for leisurely hikes or sunset views. The setting sun illuminates the park's amphitheaters, creating a breathtaking display of light and shadow.

- **Experience:** Sunset at Bryce Point is an unforgettable experience, with the sky often lighting up in shades of pink, orange, and red that reflect off the hoodoos, providing spectacular photo opportunities.

Popular Attractions

Bryce Canyon National Park is home to several must-see attractions that draw visitors from around the world. These sites are celebrated for their natural beauty and for their accessibility and the unique experiences they offer.

Bryce Amphitheater:

Housing the largest collection of hoodoos in the world, this is the most visited section of the park. Trails like the Queen's Garden and the Navajo Loop offer up-close views of the intricate formations.

Sunrise and Sunset Points:

These adjacent viewpoints are easily accessible and provide some of the most iconic views of the Bryce Amphitheater. They are especially popular at sunrise and sunset when the light plays off the hoodoos.

Thor's Hammer:

Located along the Navajo Loop, this is one of the most famous and photographed hoodoos in the park. Its striking shape makes it a favorite subject for photographers.

Inspiration Point:

Offering expansive views of the Bryce Amphitheater, Inspiration Point is accessible via a short walk from the main road and provides one of the best overlooks of the park's grandeur.

Visiting these attractions, especially with strategic timing and on less crowded days, can significantly enhance your enjoyment and appreciation of Bryce Canyon National Park.

Exploring Lesser-Known Areas

While Bryce Canyon National Park is famous for its iconic hoodoos and breathtaking vistas, it also boasts several lesser-known areas that offer stunning beauty without the crowds. Exploring these quieter parts of the park can provide a more serene experience.

Cathedral Valley:

Located in the northern reaches of Capitol Reef National Park, Cathedral Valley is known for its monolithic sandstone formations that resemble cathedrals. This area requires a high-clearance vehicle to navigate the rugged roads, which deters many visitors, making it a perfect spot for those seeking solitude. Key sights include the Temple of the Sun and Temple of the Moon, which provide dramatic photographic opportunities, especially at sunrise and sunset.

Waterpocket Fold:

The Waterpocket Fold in Capitol Reef is a geologic monocline extending nearly 100 miles. Due to its remote location and lack of developed trails, it is less frequented by visitors, but it offers remarkable hiking opportunities and stunning geological formations. Notable areas include the Strike Valley Overlook and the Burro Wash slot canyon, which provides an adventurous hike through narrow, twisting corridors.

Sample Itineraries for Crowded Days

When visiting Bryce Canyon National Park during peak visitor times, having a well-structured itinerary can help you avoid the busiest areas and make the most of your visit.

Morning:

- Start your day early by heading to Sunrise Point to watch the sunrise illuminate the amphitheater—an early start beats the crowds and catches the best light for photography.

- After sunrise, take the Fairyland Loop Trail, which is less crowded than the main amphitheater trails. This 8-mile loop offers spectacular views and a more tranquil hiking experience.

Midday:

- Avoid the park's central areas during midday when they are most crowded. Instead, drive to the southern end of the park to explore less crowded sites like Rainbow Point and Yovimpa Point. These viewpoints offer expansive views of the park and the Grand Staircase region beyond.

Afternoon:

- As the afternoon progresses and the crowds begin to thin, consider a visit to Mossy Cave on the park's northeast side. This area features a short walk leading to a waterfall and a moss-covered cave, and it's typically less crowded than the main park areas.

Flexible Itinerary Ideas

Flexibility can greatly enhance your experience at Bryce Canyon, especially during busy days. Here are some suggestions based on crowd levels:

High Crowd Levels:

If the park feels overwhelmingly busy, consider taking a scenic drive along Highway 12 through the Grand Staircase-Escalante National Monument. This area offers numerous pullouts with spectacular views and less foot traffic.

Moderate Crowd Levels:

Keep an eye on the shuttle stops; if you notice less activity at a particular stop, take the opportunity to explore that area. The Bristlecone Loop at Rainbow Point is often less crowded and offers a quiet walk through ancient Bristlecone pine forests.

Low Crowd Levels:

Take advantage of the rare quiet moments in popular areas like the Navajo Loop or the Rim Trail near Sunset Point. If these areas are less crowded than usual, they provide a wonderful, unhurried experience of the park's most famous sights.

By tailoring your visit according to these strategies, you can navigate Bryce Canyon National Park more effectively, ensuring a memorable and enjoyable experience even on the busiest days.

Off-the-Beaten-Path Hikes

For those willing to step off the well-trodden path, Bryce Canyon National Park and its environs offer several less-known hikes that are as stunning as they are solitary. Here are some recommended trails:

Cassidy Arch Trail (Capitol Reef National Park):

While technically located in Capitol Reef, about a two-hour drive from Bryce, the Cassidy Arch Trail merits a visit for its impressive sandstone arch, named after the infamous outlaw Butch Cassidy. This moderately challenging hike rewards adventurers with breathtaking views from the arch, set against the striking geological backdrop of Capitol Reef's Waterpocket Fold.

Hat Shop Trail:

Located within Bryce Canyon, this under-visited trail descends from Bryce Point and offers a unique perspective on the park's famous hoodoos. The trail is named for its hoodoos topped with boulders that resemble hats. This 4-mile round trip provides a quiet, immersive experience in the park's surreal landscape.

Riggs Spring Loop Trail:

This 8.5-mile loop trail offers solitude and the chance to explore Bryce's backcountry. It descends from Yovimpa Point through a mix of forest and red rock scenery, with overnight camping options for those looking to extend their adventure.

Wildlife Viewing and Nature Photography

Bryce Canyon and surrounding areas are teeming with wildlife, providing excellent opportunities for viewing and photography. Here are some best practices to ensure respectful and successful wildlife encounters:

Maintain Distance:

Always keep a safe distance from wildlife to avoid stress and disruption to their natural behaviors. Use binoculars and telephoto lenses to observe or photograph from afar.

Minimize Noise:

Move quietly and speak softly when near wildlife. Sudden sounds can startle animals, causing them stress and potentially provoking aggression.

Use Natural Light:

For photography, take advantage of the golden hours of early morning and late afternoon when light is soft and animals are more active. Avoid using flash, which can disorient and disturb wildlife.

Stay on Trails:

Stick to designated trails to minimize impact on wildlife habitats. Venturing off-trail can damage sensitive vegetation and disturb animal homes.

Be Patient and Prepared:

Wildlife viewing often requires patience. Spend time quietly waiting and watching. Always be prepared with the right gear, and never attempt to attract wildlife with food or calls.

Stargazing Opportunities

Bryce Canyon is renowned for its dark skies, making it an ideal destination for stargazing. Here are tips to enhance your night sky viewing:

Plan Around the Moon:

Check the lunar calendar and plan your stargazing during the new moon when the sky is darkest. Avoid full moon nights, as the moonlight can wash out dimmer stars.

Find a Dark Spot:

While Bryce itself is a Dark Sky Park, seek out locations like Farview Point or the end of the Fairyland Loop Trail for especially dark conditions away from any possible light pollution from the visitor center or parking lots.

Join a Ranger Program:

Bryce Canyon offers ranger-led night sky programs that enhance your experience by providing insights into astronomy and the chance to look through large telescopes.

Bring the Right Equipment:

A star chart or stargazing app can help you identify constellations and celestial events. Binoculars or a telescope will allow you to see more detail, such as the rings of Saturn or the moons of Jupiter.

Prepare for Nighttime Conditions:

Nights at high elevations can be cold, even in summer. Dress warmly, bring a comfortable chair or a blanket, and pack some hot drinks to stay warm as you gaze up at the stars.

By following these guidelines, your experience exploring the quieter trails, observing wildlife, and stargazing in Bryce Canyon can be both fulfilling and respectful to the natural environment.

Where to Stay

While visiting Bryce Canyon National Park, staying in nearby towns can enhance your experience by offering serene escapes from the park's busier areas. Here are several excellent lodging options that provide comfort and convenience while avoiding the crowds:

Panguitch:

Located just 30 minutes from Bryce Canyon, Panguitch is a charming town with a selection of motels, bed and breakfasts, and historic inns that capture the spirit of the Old West.

- **The Panguitch House:** A cozy bed and breakfast known for its friendly service and home-like atmosphere, ideal for those seeking a quiet retreat.

- **Blue Pine Motel:** Offers comfortable, family-friendly accommodations with easy access to both Bryce Canyon and nearby scenic attractions.

Tropic:

Tropic is another excellent option for visitors looking to stay close to Bryce Canyon while enjoying a small-town atmosphere.

- **Bryce Canyon Inn Cabins:** Providing private cabins that offer a more secluded lodging experience, perfect for those who prefer a bit of solitude.

- **Stone Canyon Inn:** Features spacious rooms and stunning views of the surrounding landscapes, with easy access to the park.

Cannonville:

A few minutes further from Bryce than Tropic, Cannonville is a quiet base for exploring the area.

- **Grand Staircase Inn:** A budget-friendly option with clean, comfortable rooms and a convenient location for visiting both Bryce Canyon and Grand Staircase-Escalante National Monument.

Escalante:

Located about an hour from Bryce, Escalante offers a range of lodging options in a less touristy setting, perfect for those looking to explore the expansive Grand Staircase-Escalante area as well as Bryce.

- **Escalante Outfitters Cabins:** Ideal for outdoor enthusiasts, these cabins provide a rustic yet comfortable place to stay with the bonus of an on-site café known for its excellent pizzas and local beer.

Dining Recommendations

Dining in the local towns near Bryce Canyon National Park can be a delightful part of your visit, especially when you choose places that are popular with residents rather than tourists. Here are some top picks:

Panguitch:

- **Cowboy's Smokehouse Café:** A favorite among locals and tourists alike, offering a range of smoked meats and traditional Western dishes in a rustic setting.

- **Henrie's Drive-In:** Perfect for grabbing a quick, tasty burger and shake, Henrie's is a hit for those looking for classic American fast food with a home-cooked quality.

Tropic:

- **IDK BBQ:** Celebrated for serving some of the best barbecues in the area, IDK BBQ is a must-visit for dinner after a long day of hiking.

- **The Stone Hearth Grille:** Offers a slightly more upscale dining experience with dishes that focus on local ingredients and flavors.

Escalante:

- **Escalante Mercantile & Natural Grocery:** Great for picking up healthy, organic foods if you prefer to prepare your own meals or need snacks for the trail.

- **Circle D Eatery:** Known for its friendly service and extensive menu, including hearty breakfasts to start your day and satisfying dinners to end it.

These options provide a taste of local cuisine and contribute to a more authentic travel experience, allowing you to enjoy regional flavors and hospitality away from the crowded park areas.

Moab

Moab, Utah, is not just a town but a gateway to some of the most striking landscapes in the American Southwest. Located near both Arches and Canyonlands National Parks, Moab serves as a base camp for adventurers drawn to its red rock vistas, towering arches, and dramatic canyons. This vibrant town is synonymous with outdoor recreation, offering everything from mountain biking and rock climbing to river rafting and off-roading.

Geological Features

Moab's landscape is a showcase of extraordinary geological formations, primarily shaped by the forces of erosion. The area is renowned for its:

Arches National Park:

The area is home to over 2,000 natural stone arches, the most famous being Delicate Arch. These arches have been sculpted over millions of years from the evaporation and precipitation of ancient seas, followed by extensive erosion from wind and water.

Canyonlands National Park:

It features a diverse landscape that includes towering rock pinnacles, deep canyons, and mesas. The Green and Colorado rivers have carved two large canyons into layers of sedimentary rock, creating wild, rugged terrain that is a dream for photographers and adventurers alike.

Dead Horse Point State Park:

Offers a spectacular view of the Colorado River and Canyonlands' intricate system of canyons. The park's dramatic overlook provides a vista that encapsulates the beauty and scale of the high desert.

The geological processes visible in Moab are a textbook example of desert landscapes formed by sedimentary deposits, followed by uplift and erosion, creating the layered rock formations visible today.

Historical Significance

Moab's history is deeply intertwined with both its cultural heritage and geological significance. Ancient Puebloans inhabited the region thousands of years ago, leaving behind rock art and dwellings that suggest a sophisticated understanding of agriculture and astronomy. Following them, the Ute and Navajo tribes inhabited the area.

In the late 19th century, Mormon settlers established the town of Moab. In the 1950s, a uranium boom brought a rush of prospectors to the area, influenced by the Cold War demand.

Today, Moab's economy is largely driven by tourism, with visitors drawn to its unique landscapes and recreational opportunities.

Off-Peak Seasons

Visiting Moab during off-peak seasons can greatly enhance the experience due to fewer crowds and a more laid-back atmosphere:

Late Fall:

Offers cooler temperatures and fewer tourists. The changing colors of the vegetation provide a beautiful contrast against the red rock.

Winter:

While it can be cold, the winter months see the least amount of tourism traffic. Snow dusting the red rocks can offer a unique and quiet beauty, ideal for photography.

Early Spring:

Early spring can be an excellent time to explore Moab before the spring break crowds arrive. Temperatures are mild, and the melting snow from the La Sal Mountains feeds the streams, creating lush landscapes.

Visiting during these seasons provides a more tranquil visit and offers a different perspective on the area's stunning geological features.

Weekday vs. Weekend Visits

Opting for a weekday visit to Moab and its surrounding parks can profoundly enhance the visitor experience, offering several advantages over the more crowded weekends:

Reduced Crowds:

Weekdays typically see significantly fewer tourists, which means shorter lines at popular attractions, less crowded trails, and more open spaces at scenic overlooks. This reduction allows for a more leisurely pace to explore and enjoy the natural beauty without feeling rushed.

Increased Availability:

Accommodations, guided tours, and recreational equipment rentals are more readily available and sometimes cheaper during weekdays. Restaurants and local amenities in Moab also tend to be less crowded, offering better service and a more relaxed atmosphere.

Enhanced Wildlife Viewing:

On weekdays, wildlife is more active and easier to spot due to fewer disturbances. This makes for excellent opportunities for wildlife photography and observation, especially in the early morning or late evening.

More Enjoyable Recreational Activities:

Outdoor activities such as biking, off-roading, and rafting can be fully enjoyed with less traffic on the trails and waterways, providing a more authentic adventure experience.

Time of Day Strategies

Choosing the right time of day for visits to Moab and its national parks is crucial, particularly for those looking to avoid the heat and capture the beauty of the landscape in the best light:

Early Morning:

- **Benefits:** The morning is the ideal time for hiking and photography. The soft, diffused light enhances the red rock formations, and temperatures are cooler, making physical activities more comfortable.

- **Experience:** Trails like Delicate Arch or Mesa Arch are perfect for sunrise viewings, offering spectacular photo opportunities as the sun illuminates the arches from beneath the horizon.

Late Afternoon and Sunset:

- **Benefits:** As the sun begins to set, Moab's landscape transforms. The red rocks glow fiercely under the golden hour light, providing a stunning backdrop for photographers and sightseers.

- **Experience:** Locations such as Dead Horse Point State Park offer unmatched sunset views, where the setting sun casts dramatic shadows and lights the winding Colorado River below.

Popular Attractions

Moab is the gateway to some of the most popular attractions in the American Southwest, drawing visitors to its unique landscape formations and outdoor adventures:

Arches National Park:

The park is known for its incredible natural arches, with Delicate Arch being the most iconic and photographed. It offers various hikes that range from easy to strenuous, accommodating all levels of adventurers.

Canyonlands National Park:

It is divided into three districts: Island in the Sky, The Needles, and The Maze. Island in the Sky is the most accessible, with panoramic overlooks like Grand View Point. The Needles offers more challenging backcountry adventures.

Corona Arch:

Outside of the national parks, Corona Arch is a popular free-standing arch that rivals those found within Arches National Park. It's accessible via a moderate hike and is less regulated than the national parks, offering a different type of adventure.

By visiting these attractions with strategic timing and choosing weekdays, visitors can maximize their experience in Moab, enjoying the natural wonders in relative solitude and capturing moments of quiet beauty in this extraordinary desert landscape.

Exploring Lesser-Known Areas

While Moab is synonymous with Arches and Canyonlands, numerous lesser-known areas offer stunning beauty without the crowds. These locations provide tranquil alternatives for visitors seeking solitude and unspoiled nature.

Cathedral Valley (Capitol Reef National Park):

Tucked away in the northern part of Capitol Reef, Cathedral Valley is renowned for its monolithic sandstone formations that resemble cathedrals. This remote area requires a high-clearance vehicle to navigate the loop, which deters many casual tourists, ensuring a peaceful experience. Highlights include the Temple of the Sun and Temple of the Moon, massive stone structures that rise dramatically from the desert floor.

Waterpocket Fold (Capitol Reef National Park):

The Waterpocket Fold is a 100-mile-long buckle in the earth's surface. Due to its remote accessibility, it is less traveled and offers remarkable hiking opportunities and stunning geological formations. Noteworthy trails include the Strike Valley Overlook and the slot canyons of Burro Wash, Cottonwood Wash, and Sheets Gulch, which provide immersive experiences in the rugged landscape.

Sample Itineraries for Crowded Days

When visiting Moab during peak tourist seasons, a well-planned itinerary is essential to avoid congested areas and maximize enjoyment. Here's how you can structure your day:

Morning:

- Start your day early by hiking to less popular but equally stunning trails such as the Fisher Towers or Morning Glory Natural Bridge. These areas tend to be less crowded, especially in the early hours, allowing for a serene hiking experience.

Midday:

- As the larger crowds start to move towards the popular parks around midday, take a scenic drive along the Upper Colorado River Scenic Byway (Route 128). This route offers numerous stops with breathtaking views and riverside picnic spots for a relaxing lunch away from the crowds.

Afternoon:

- In the late afternoon, explore areas in Canyonlands' Island in the Sky district, such as the Aztec Butte or Upheaval Dome. These trails are often less busy later in the day and provide spectacular sunset vistas.

Flexible Itinerary Ideas

Adapting to crowd levels can greatly enhance your experience in Moab. Here are flexible itinerary ideas based on real-time conditions:

High Crowd Levels:

- If Arches or Canyonlands feels overcrowded, consider visiting Dead Horse Point State Park. It offers majestic views of the Colorado River and the surrounding canyon country with fewer visitors.

Moderate Crowd Levels:

- Monitor parking availability via park apps or websites. If popular spots are filling up, head to areas like Klondike Bluffs or Tower Arch in the northern section of Arches, which are typically less crowded.

Low Crowd Levels:

- Take advantage of the rare quiet moments at popular sites. If you find that main attractions like Delicate Arch have fewer visitors than usual, seize the opportunity for a quieter visit to these iconic landmarks.

By staying flexible and prepared, you can comfortably enjoy Moab's natural wonders, even on busy days, ensuring a memorable and enjoyable adventure in this spectacular region.

Off-the-Beaten-Path Hikes

For those looking to escape the crowds and delve into quieter realms, several lesser-known trails in and around Moab offer tranquility and stunning natural beauty:

Hidden Valley Trail:

Nestled just south of Moab, the Hidden Valley Trail offers a serene escape into a secluded valley flanked by towering sandstone cliffs. This moderately challenging hike covers approximately 4 miles round trip and rewards hikers with ancient petroglyphs and expansive views of the Moab Valley and Behind the Rocks Wilderness Study Area.

Stairmaster Trail (Canyonlands National Park):

Located in the lesser-visited Maze District of Canyonlands, the Stairmaster Trail offers a rigorous adventure to those looking for isolation and spectacular canyon views. This trail is not well-marked and requires good navigation skills, making it a perfect match for experienced hikers seeking solitude.

Fisher Towers Trail:

The Fisher Towers Trail is about a 45-minute drive from Moab and offers one of the most breathtaking red rock landscapes outside of the national parks. This 4.4-mile round-trip trail winds through dramatic rock formations and spires, including the iconic Fisher Towers, famous among rock climbers.

Wildlife Viewing and Nature Photography

The diverse ecosystems around Moab provide excellent opportunities for wildlife viewing and nature photography. Here are best practices to ensure respectful and impactful encounters:

Maintain a Safe Distance:

Always keep a safe distance from animals to avoid distress and disruption of their natural behaviors. Use binoculars and telephoto lenses for safe observation and photography.

Be Patient and Quiet:

Patience is key in wildlife viewing and photography. Spend time quietly waiting at likely spots such as water sources early in the morning or late in the evening. Minimize noise and sudden movements to avoid scaring wildlife away.

Use Natural Lighting:

Utilize the soft light of early mornings and late afternoons for photography. These times provide the best light for highlighting the textures and colors of wildlife and coincide with peak animal activity.

Respect Their Space:

Encroaching on wildlife habitat spaces, especially nesting or breeding areas, should be avoided. To minimize impact, stick to trails and public areas.

No Baiting:

Do not use calls, lures, or bait to attract animals. Such practices can alter natural behaviors and potentially put both the wildlife and yourself at risk.

Stargazing Opportunities

Moab's remote location away from major light pollution sources makes it an exceptional spot for stargazing. Here are tips to enhance your night-sky viewing:

Choose Dark Locations:

Drive away from the light pollution of Moab town to darker areas such as Arches National Park or Dead Horse Point State Park. These locations offer some of the darkest skies and most unobstructed celestial views.

New Moon Nights:

Plan your stargazing trips during the new moon phase when the sky is darkest. Avoid times around the full moon, which can wash out dimmer stars.

Acclimate Your Eyes:

Allow your eyes 20-30 minutes to adjust to the dark for optimal night vision. Use red lights instead of standard flashlights or headlamps to maintain night vision.

Use Apps and Maps:

Astronomical apps and star maps can enhance your experience by helping you identify stars, planets, and constellations. Some apps also provide augmented reality star charting.

By following these guidelines, you can enjoy Moab's remarkable natural and celestial landscapes responsibly, ensuring a rewarding experience in the great outdoors.

Where to Stay

While Moab itself offers numerous lodging options, staying in smaller towns nearby can provide a quieter, more secluded experience. Here are some great choices for accommodations away from the typical tourist spots:

Torrey, Utah:

- **Capitol Reef Resort:** Just a few miles from Capitol Reef National Park, this resort offers comfortable lodging with stunning views of the red rock cliffs. Guests can choose from traditional hotel rooms, cabins, and even covered wagons for a unique overnight experience.

- **Broken Spur Inn:** Known for its Western charm and hospitality, the Broken Spur Inn provides spacious rooms and includes amenities like a hot tub and pool, which are ideal for relaxing after a day of adventures.

Green River, Utah:

- **River Terrace Inn:** Offering serene river views and excellent customer service, the River Terrace Inn in Green River is perfect for those looking to escape the Moab crowds. It's about a 45-minute drive to Moab but provides easy access to both Arches and Canyonlands.

- **Budget Inn:** For a more economical stay without sacrificing cleanliness and comfort, the Budget Inn is a good choice, especially for travelers looking to extend their stay in the area.

Blanding, Utah:

- **Stone Lizard Lodging:** Nestled in the quiet town of Blanding, this quaint lodging option offers a comfortable stay with easy access to natural attractions like Natural Bridges National Monument and the edges of Bears Ears National Monument.

- **Four Corners Inn:** Providing simple, clean accommodations, Four Corners Inn is an excellent base for exploring Utah's southeastern part, including Monument Valley and the San Juan River.

Dining Recommendations

Exploring local eateries that are favored by residents rather than just catering to tourists can offer a more authentic and enjoyable dining experience. Here are some recommended spots:

Moab:

- **Moab Brewery:** While still popular among tourists, Moab Brewery offers a local vibe. It has an excellent selection of craft beers brewed on-site and a diverse menu that includes everything from burgers to vegan options.

- **Milt's Stop & Eat:** Since 1954, Milt's has been serving locals. It offers delicious, no-fuss diner fare and is Moab's oldest operating restaurant. Don't miss their famous milkshakes and locally sourced beef burgers.

Green River:

- **Ray's Tavern:** A local favorite for over 50 years, Ray's Tavern is known for its friendly atmosphere and great selection of grilled items, making it a perfect stop for travelers coming from or heading to Moab.

- **Tamarisk Restaurant:** Located on the banks of the Green River, Tamarisk Restaurant offers scenic views along with a menu that features a good mix of American and Southwestern dishes.

Torrey:

- **Slackers Burger Joint:** Known for their tasty burgers and casual setting, Slackers is a favorite among both locals and visitors staying in or passing through Torrey.

- **Café Diablo:** Offers innovative Southwestern cuisine with a twist. Their menu features local ingredients and creative dishes that make it a culinary landmark in the area.

By choosing these lodging and dining options, you can enjoy a more relaxed atmosphere while still having easy access to Utah's stunning natural landscapes and vibrant local culture.

Arches National Park

Arches National Park, located just north of Moab, Utah, is a red rock wonderland with over 2,000 natural stone arches, towering pinnacles, massive fins, and giant balanced rocks. This park covers approximately 76,679 acres and offers some of the most striking and picturesque landscapes in the American Southwest. The park's unique geological features have been sculpted over millions of years by the forces of nature and continue to evolve to this day.

Geological Features

Arches National Park's landscape is primarily made up of sedimentary rock, including sandstone, which has been eroded by water and wind over an immense period. The most iconic features of the park are its natural arches, which vary in size and shape and include famous formations such as Delicate Arch, Landscape Arch, and Double Arch. These natural structures are the result of a combination of factors, including the uneven deposition of sands and salts, extreme temperatures, and particular rock permeability.

Beyond the arches, the park is also home to other fascinating geological formations:

- **Fins:** Narrow walls of rock that are formed when water infiltrates large cracks in the sandstone, expanding and contracting with the thermal cycles, eventually causing chunks of rock to fall away.

- **Pinnacles:** Pointed spires of rock that are remnants of sandstone layers that have further eroded from fins.

- **Balanced Rocks:** Large boulders that have eroded in such a way that they balance precariously on a narrow pedestal, exemplified by the park's famous Balanced Rock.

These features create an almost surreal landscape, offering an array of formations that play with light and shadow under the Utah sun. From sunrise to sunset, these features provide spectacular views and photo opportunities.

Historical Significance

Arches National Park has a deep historical and cultural significance, marked by the presence of various indigenous tribes over thousands of years. The area was originally home to the Puebloans, whose petroglyphs and pictographs are still visible within the park today, providing insight into their lifestyle and culture. Later, the Ute and Paiute tribes frequented the region.

The park's modern history began with its designation as a national monument in 1929 under President Herbert Hoover and was later re-designated as a national park in 1971. The park has attracted countless visitors and inspired many with its majestic landscapes and the stories of those who lived here and those who have worked to preserve its natural beauty.

Off-Peak Seasons

Visiting Arches National Park during the off-peak seasons can greatly enhance the experience by providing a more solitary exploration of its wonders:

- **Late Fall:** The weather is cooler, and the summer crowds have dwindled, making it a perfect time to explore the park in peace.

- **Winter:** Snowfall is rare but possible, and it beautifully contrasts with the red rock, offering unique and quiet winter landscapes. Fewer visitors during this time mean you can enjoy popular spots without the crowds.

- **Early Spring:** Before the influx of spring break visitors, the park experiences a gentle reawakening with comfortable temperatures and blooming desert flowers.

These seasons offer the solitude many seek and unique perspectives of the park's ever-changing landscape, free from the intense heat and congestion of peak tourist periods.

Weekday vs. Weekend Visits

Opting to visit Arches National Park on weekdays rather than weekends offers several benefits that can significantly enhance your experience:

- **Reduced Crowds:** Weekdays typically see fewer visitors, making popular sites like Delicate Arch, Windows Section, and Devil's Garden less congested. You'll have more freedom to explore at your own pace without waiting for parking spots or navigating through large groups on trails.

- **Easier Parking Access:** Parking can be a significant issue at Arches, especially during peak times. On weekends, lots at popular trailheads often fill up quickly, while on weekdays, it's much easier to secure a spot close to the attractions you want to see.

- **Better Wildlife Viewing Opportunities:** With fewer visitors, animals are more likely to be active and visible. Visiting on a quieter weekday increases your chances of encountering wildlife such as mule deer, desert cottontails, and various bird species.

- **Enhanced Photography and Viewing Experience:** Weekdays provide more uninterrupted views, making it easier to capture the stunning rock formations without crowds in the frame. You'll have time to set up your shots and fully enjoy the park's breathtaking beauty.

Time of Day Strategies

Selecting the right time of day for your visit can make a world of difference, particularly when it comes to avoiding the heat and capturing the landscape in the best light.

Early Morning:

- **Benefits:** Early morning is the ideal time to explore the park, with cooler temperatures and softer light. The rock formations glow in warm tones as the sun rises, creating incredible photographic opportunities.

- **Experience:** Trails like Delicate Arch and the Windows Section are especially beautiful at sunrise, and these areas are less crowded in the morning, allowing you to fully immerse yourself in the serene environment.

Late Afternoon and Sunset:

- **Benefits:** As the sun begins to set, the temperature cools, and the park's rock formations become even more vibrant under the warm hues of the setting sun. Late afternoon and sunset provide excellent lighting for photography and a quieter, more relaxed atmosphere.

- **Experience:** Balanced Rock, the Windows, and Park Avenue are great places to visit in the evening, where you can witness the rocks' colors deepening under the golden hour light.

Popular Attractions

Arches National Park is home to several iconic attractions that draw visitors from all over the world:

Delicate Arch:

- The most famous arch in the park and one of the most recognized natural landmarks in the U.S. The 3-mile round-trip hike to Delicate Arch offers rewarding views, with the arch framed by the La Sal Mountains in the background.

Windows Section and Double Arch:

- This area features several impressive arches close together, including North Window, South Window, and Double Arch. It's accessible via a short hike and offers some of the park's best views for sunrise and sunset.

Devil's Garden and Landscape Arch:

- The Devil's Garden Trail leads to the longest arch in North America, Landscape Arch, along with several other stunning formations, such as Double O Arch and Partition Arch. For those wanting to explore even further, the trail can be extended into a more challenging hike.

Balanced Rock:

- One of the park's most photographed formations, Balanced Rock is easily accessible and offers a unique, close-up view of this precarious formation that seems to defy gravity.

Visiting these popular attractions on weekdays and at strategic times of the day can enhance your experience by reducing crowd interactions and providing optimal lighting for viewing and photography.

Exploring Lesser-Known Areas

Arches National Park is famous for its iconic formations, but venturing beyond the popular sites reveals lesser-known areas that offer equally awe-inspiring views with fewer visitors:

Tower Arch Trail:

- Located in the park's remote Klondike Bluffs area, the Tower Arch Trail provides a 3.4-mile round-trip hike through unique rock formations and sand dunes to the impressive Tower Arch. The trail is moderately challenging, with some rocky sections, but rewards hikers with solitude and spectacular views of this massive, hidden arch.

Sand Dune Arch and Broken Arch:

- Although these arches are relatively accessible, they are less frequented than the Delicate Arch and the Windows. Sand Dune Arch is located in a small, sandy slot canyon, making it a perfect spot for shade and photography. A short hike from Sand Dune Arch leads to Broken Arch, offering expansive views of the surrounding landscape.

Courthouse Wash Rock Art Panel:

- This area combines natural beauty with cultural history. Located near the park entrance, the Courthouse Wash Rock Art Panel features ancient Native American petroglyphs. The short, less-traveled hike to the panel provides a quiet and culturally enriching experience.

Park Avenue Trail:

- Though close to the entrance, this trail is often overlooked by visitors heading straight to the main arches. Park Avenue is a 2-mile round-trip hike through a canyon flanked by towering rock walls and monoliths, resembling a desert cityscape. The unique rock formations here offer beautiful photo opportunities, especially in the early morning light.

Sample Itineraries for Crowded Days

Planning a structured itinerary on crowded days can help you experience the best of Arches while avoiding peak areas:

Morning:

- Start early with a hike to Delicate Arch, arriving just before sunrise to avoid crowds. This timing reduces foot traffic and provides stunning light for photos.

- After the hike, head to the Sand Dune Arch area. This section is often less crowded and shaded, making it a refreshing stop as the day warms up.

Midday:

- During the busiest hours, take a scenic drive through the park's quieter areas, such as Courthouse Towers and Fiery Furnace Viewpoint. Pack a lunch and enjoy a peaceful picnic at one of the park's designated areas.

Afternoon:

- In the late afternoon, explore the Tower Arch Trail or Park Avenue Trail. These areas tend to be quieter, and the afternoon light casts beautiful shadows across the rock formations.

Flexible Itinerary Ideas

A flexible itinerary can help you adapt to varying crowd levels, allowing you to explore Arches comfortably, even on busy days:

High Crowd Levels:

- If popular areas are too crowded, consider visiting nearby Dead Horse Point State Park. This park offers breathtaking canyon views with much smaller crowds and is just a short drive from Arches.

Moderate Crowd Levels:

- Keep an eye on the parking lots and trail activity. If you notice fewer people in a particular area, take advantage of it. The Devil's Garden Trail offers several options to adjust based on crowd levels, allowing you to explore part or all of the trail, including less-visited sections like Navajo Arch and Partition Arch.

Low Crowd Levels:

- Explore main attractions like the Windows Section or Delicate Arch during the rare moments when the park is less crowded. You'll be able to fully enjoy these iconic formations without feeling rushed or surrounded by other visitors.

With these strategies, you can navigate Arches National Park effectively, even on busier days, ensuring a rewarding and memorable experience while minimizing your interactions with crowds.

Off-the-Beaten-Path Hikes

While Arches National Park is famous for the Delicate Arch and the Windows, exploring less frequented trails offers a serene experience with equally spectacular scenery:

Tower Arch Trail:

Located in the Klondike Bluffs area, the 3.4-mile round-trip Tower Arch Trail provides a peaceful alternative to the busier trails. The path winds through sandy washes, small dunes, and striking sandstone fins before arriving at the massive Tower Arch. This trail requires a bit of effort, with some scrambling over rocks, but the solitude and the arch's grandeur make it well worth it.

Primitive Loop Trail in Devil's Garden:

For a more challenging, less-traveled route, try the Primitive Loop Trail in Devil's Garden. This 7.2-mile loop connects with the main trail but takes you through rugged landscapes and offers views of unique formations like Dark Angel. The narrow ledges, sandy terrain, and rock scrambles make this trail ideal for experienced hikers seeking a quieter adventure.

Broken Arch Trail:

Accessed from the Sand Dune Arch Trailhead, this moderate 1.7-mile loop leads to Broken Arch. This trail offers an up-close experience with classic rock formations and the chance to wander through a quiet meadow. The natural archway view at the end is a rewarding sight, especially in the soft light of early morning or late afternoon.

Wildlife Viewing and Nature Photography

Arches National Park is home to a variety of wildlife, including desert bighorn sheep, mule deer, and numerous bird species. Here are some best practices for observing and photographing wildlife responsibly:

Keep a Safe Distance:

Always observe wildlife from a safe distance to avoid causing stress or disruption. Use binoculars or telephoto lenses for close-up shots without encroaching on their space.

Minimize Noise and Movements:

Move slowly and quietly to avoid startling animals. Speak softly if needed, and avoid sudden movements that might scare wildlife away.

Use Natural Light:

The soft lighting of early morning or late afternoon enhances photography and aligns with times when animals are most active. Avoid using flash, which can disturb animals and disrupt natural behaviors.

Stay on Designated Paths:

Avoid off-trail excursions when observing wildlife to minimize habitat disruption and protect fragile desert ecosystems. Stick to established paths to preserve animal habitats.

Avoid Feeding or Attracting Wildlife:

Feeding wildlife is prohibited, as it can alter natural behaviors and lead to dependency on human food, which can be harmful to their health.

Stargazing Opportunities

Arches National Park's remote location and dark skies make it a top destination for stargazing. Here are tips for an unforgettable night under the stars:

Plan Around the Moon Cycle:

- Visit during a new moon for the darkest skies. Moonlight can obscure the view of fainter stars and celestial objects, so aim for nights when the moon is less visible.

Head to Darker Spots:

- Popular stargazing locations include Balanced Rock, The Windows, and Panorama Point, where light pollution is minimal. These spots offer clear, expansive views of the sky with iconic rock formations as a silhouette backdrop.

Use Red Lights to Preserve Night Vision:

- To maintain night vision, bring a flashlight or headlamp with a red light setting. Red lights are less intrusive and help your eyes adjust to the dark more quickly.

Bring Binoculars or a Telescope:

- While the naked eye can capture stunning views, binoculars or a small telescope can reveal even more, including Jupiter's moons, Saturn's rings, and distant galaxies.

Dress in Layers:

- Desert nights can be surprisingly cold, even in warmer months, so dress in layers and bring blankets or chairs for comfortable viewing.

Following these tips will enhance your experience on less-traveled hikes, allow for responsible wildlife viewing, and create magical stargazing memories in one of America's most breathtaking national parks.

Where to Stay

Staying outside Arches National Park offers a more peaceful experience and can be a great way to explore other nearby attractions without the crowds. Here are some recommended towns and accommodations for a quieter, relaxing stay:

Moab:

Though Moab is close to the park, staying in quieter parts of town or at less-centralized lodgings can provide a more restful experience.

- **Red Cliffs Lodge:** Located along the Colorado River about 15 miles from Moab, Red Cliffs Lodge offers scenic views, cozy cabins, and horseback riding, all in a more secluded environment.

- **Sorrel River Ranch Resort:** A luxury option set away from the main town, with breathtaking river views, farm-to-table dining, and private cabins that offer a peaceful retreat after a day of adventure.

Green River:

About 50 minutes from Arches, Green River is a small town with easy access to both Arches and Canyonlands and a quieter environment.

- **River Terrace Inn:** Known for its riverfront views, friendly service, and beautiful garden, this inn offers a calm escape with close access to Green River State Park.

- **Holiday Inn Express Green River:** A comfortable and convenient option with modern amenities, perfect for families or travelers looking for affordable comfort and a short drive to the parks.

Torrey:

Situated near Capitol Reef National Park and about 1.5 hours from Moab, Torrey is ideal if you're looking to explore beyond Arches.

- **Capitol Reef Resort:** With stunning views of red rock formations, this resort offers a variety of accommodations, including teepees and Conestoga wagons, creating a unique lodging experience.

- **Broken Spur Inn & Steakhouse:** Known for its Western charm and friendly service, this inn provides rustic comfort, a steakhouse on-site, and convenient access to Capitol Reef.

Dining Recommendations

For a taste of local flavor away from the usual tourist spots, here are some hidden gems where you can enjoy excellent food with a more relaxed atmosphere:

Moab:

- **Milt's Stop & Eat:** Established in 1954, Milt's is Moab's oldest diner, offering delicious burgers, hand-cut fries, and milkshakes. The casual, old-school vibe is perfect for a low-key meal loved by locals.

- **98 Center:** Known for its locally sourced, creative dishes with an Asian-Southwestern fusion, 98 Center is a gem for fresh, flavorful food in a relaxed atmosphere. They're famous for their pho and unique vegetarian options.

Green River:

- **Ray's Tavern:** A no-frills, classic American tavern that's a favorite among locals and travelers alike. Ray's serves up hearty burgers, steaks, and sandwiches, with a laid-back vibe and cold beer to cap off a day of exploration.

- **Tamarisk Restaurant:** With a view of the Green River, Tamarisk offers a broad menu that includes comfort food classics and Southwestern dishes. Its scenic riverside location provides a perfect escape from the busy parks.

Torrey:

- **Café Diablo:** This popular spot in Torrey offers upscale Southwestern cuisine in a casual, artsy environment. Known for its creative use of local ingredients, Café Diablo is a must-visit for foodies.

- **Capitol Burger:** Located on Torrey's main strip, this small, family-run burger joint serves up freshly made burgers with locally sourced ingredients, making it a hit with both locals and visitors.

These lodging and dining options provide a mix of comfort, local charm, and unique experiences, making your trip to Arches and the surrounding areas both memorable and relaxing.

CHAPTER 4

Smart Itinerary Planning

Planning a trip to iconic destinations like Arches National Park and the surrounding areas requires more than just checking off the highlights. A well-thought-out itinerary can transform your experience, helping you avoid the crowds, enjoy hidden gems, and create unforgettable moments. Smart itinerary planning isn't just about hitting the popular spots; it's about balancing must-see locations with quieter, lesser-known places, all while factoring in time, weather, and personal energy levels.

In this chapter, we'll dive into practical strategies to help you build a flexible, rewarding itinerary. From choosing the best times to visit popular areas to including off-the-beaten-path hikes, these tips are designed to make your trip as enjoyable and seamless as possible. You'll learn how to plan around peak crowd hours, explore alternative routes, and even include downtime to appreciate the breathtaking landscapes fully.

The goal is to see the sights and feel connected to them— whether that's watching a serene sunrise over Delicate Arch, taking a quiet stroll through Tower Arch, or ending the day with stargazing in a secluded part of the park. Smart itinerary planning gives you the freedom to adapt and enjoy each moment, turning a crowded landmark into a memorable personal experience.

Let's start with the essentials of strategic timing, trail selection, and balancing must-see stops with hidden treasures. With the right plan, your journey through Arches, Canyonlands, and the greater Moab area will be a beautifully curated adventure tailored to your interests and pace.

Flexible Itinerary Suggestions

When visiting popular destinations like Arches National Park and the surrounding Moab area, crafting an itinerary that avoids the crowds while maximizing your experience is key. These flexible itinerary suggestions are designed to help you explore these stunning landscapes during less crowded times, allowing for a more personal and enjoyable visit.

Day 1: Exploring Arches National Park

Early Morning: Sunrise at Delicate Arch

- **Timing:** Arrive early (pre-sunrise) to beat the crowds and capture the iconic arch in the soft morning light.

- **Tip:** Pack breakfast to enjoy a quiet meal with a view after the sunrise.

Mid-Morning: Windows Section Mini-Hike

- **Timing:** Head here after Delicate Arch as most visitors start their day later.

- **Activity:** Explore North Window, South Window, and Turret Arch—a short loop with significant rewards and fewer people mid-morning.

Lunch: Picnic at Panorama Point

- **Relaxation:** Enjoy a packed lunch with panoramic views, avoiding crowded park restaurants or picnic areas.

Afternoon: Fiery Furnace Guided Tour

- **Adventure:** Book in advance for a ranger-led hike through the Fiery Furnace's maze-like fins and sandstone canyons. This tour limits participant numbers, ensuring a quieter experience.

Late Afternoon: Park Avenue Trail

- **Cool Down:** As the day cools, take a leisurely stroll down this less trafficked trail, enjoying the monolithic courthouse towers and three gossips.

Evening: Sunset at Balanced Rock

- **Unwind:** End your day watching the sunset illuminate Balanced Rock, a quieter evening spot perfect for reflection and photography.

Day 2: Canyonlands and Dead Horse Point

Sunrise: Mesa Arch (Canyonlands – Island in the Sky)

- **Early Start:** Catch the sunrise at Mesa Arch when it's less crowded. The early morning light creates a picturesque glow underneath the arch.

Mid-Morning: Upheaval Dome Hike

- **Exploration:** Hike to Upheaval Dome, an intriguing geological feature. The trail sees fewer visitors and offers a unique look at what might be an ancient meteorite impact site.

Lunch: Dead Horse Point State Park

- **Scenic Views:** Enjoy a scenic lunch at one of the picnic areas overlooking the Colorado River far below, a stunning alternative to the busier park spots.

Afternoon: Grand View Point

- **Leisurely Hike:** Spend your afternoon at Grand View Point, taking an easy walk along the rim for breathtaking views of the White Rim Road and the surrounding canyons.

Evening: Stargazing Near Moab

- **Night Skies:** Return to Moab and head out to a dark sky spot for some stargazing. Areas outside the national parks, like along the Colorado River Corridor, offer fantastic dark skies without the park crowds.

Day 3: Moab's Hidden Gems

Morning: Corona Arch Trail

- **Off-Park Hike:** Start with a hike to Corona Arch outside of Arches NP. This impressive arch rivals those within the park and sees fewer visitors.

Mid-Morning: Potash Road Petroglyphs

- **Cultural Insight:** Visit the petroglyphs along Potash Road, offering a glimpse into the area's ancient cultures with far fewer crowds than park attractions.

Lunch: Local Eatery in Moab

- **Local Flavor:** Enjoy lunch at a local favorite like Milt's Stop & Eat, offering great food and a slice of Moab's local scene.

Afternoon: Kayaking on the Colorado River

- **Relaxing Paddle:** Spend your afternoon kayaking or stand-up paddleboarding on a quieter section of the Colorado River, away from the usual tourist routes.

Evening: Dinner in Downtown Moab

- **Dine Local:** Conclude your trip with dinner at a less touristy restaurant, such as the 98 Center, for a unique fusion menu and to enjoy Moab's relaxed evening ambiance.

These itineraries blend early starts, strategic site selection, and off-peak attractions to ensure you enjoy the majesty of Moab and its national parks without the typical crowds. Each day is a unique adventure tailored to quieter exploration.

Time of Day Strategies

Understanding the best times to visit popular attractions can greatly enhance your experience by allowing you to enjoy magnificent views and activities with fewer crowds and optimal lighting. This chapter focuses on time-of-day strategies that leverage the natural rhythm of visitor traffic and the unique lighting conditions of the landscapes in Arches National Park and the surrounding Moab area.

Best Times to Visit Popular Attractions

Timing your visits to popular attractions can make the difference between a crowded experience and a more personal connection with the natural beauty of the area.

Delicate Arch (Arches National Park):

- **Sunrise:** Arriving at Delicate Arch for sunrise provides cooler temperatures and fewer crowds and offers a stunning natural light show as the first rays illuminate the arch.

- **Late Afternoon:** Visiting before sunset allows you to capture the changing colors of the rock as the sun sets; although this can be a more crowded time, it's worth it for the spectacular views.

Double Arch (Arches National Park):

- **Morning:** Early mornings are less crowded. The soft morning light enhances the massive, intertwined arches, making it ideal for photography.

- **Midday:** While this time can be busier, the high sun allows for dramatic lighting deep within the arches' span.

Mesa Arch (Canyonlands National Park):

- **Sunrise:** Famous for its sunrise glow, where the underside of the arch lights up with the rising sun. This time is popular with photographers, so early arrival is crucial.

The Windows Section (Arches National Park):

- **Late Afternoon to Sunset:** This time offers softer light and longer shadows, which dramatically define the arches and spires. Sunset at The Windows is less crowded than sunrise, providing a tranquil experience as the day ends.

Dead Horse Point State Park:

- **Sunrise and Sunset:** Both times are spectacular at Dead Horse Point. Sunrise illuminates the deep canyons and potash ponds, while sunset offers dramatic views of the Colorado River, turning the entire landscape into a golden spectacle.

Early Morning vs. Late Afternoon Visits

Choosing between early morning and late afternoon visits involves considering factors such as light, temperature, and personal schedule preferences. Here's how to decide the best time to explore:

Advantages of Early Morning:

- **Lighting:** The soft, diffused light of early morning enhances the red rock formations, making them vibrant and highly photogenic.

- **Cooler Temperatures:** Especially during summer, morning temperatures are more bearable, making hiking and exploration more comfortable.

- **Less Crowded:** Most visitors prefer to start their day later, so early risers enjoy quieter moments at major attractions.

Activities Suited for Early Morning:

- Hiking to popular arches like Delicate Arch or longer trails like the Devil's Garden in Arches National Park.

- Wildlife viewing, as many animals are active at dawn.

Advantages of Late Afternoon:

- **Golden Hour:** The hour before sunset, known as the golden hour, offers incredible lighting for photography. The landscape glows, and the low angle of the sun highlights textures.

- **Evening Cool Down:** As the heat of the day dissipates, late afternoon into evening becomes a pleasant time to be outside.

- **Sunset Views:** Watching the sunset transform the sky and landscape is a perfect way to end a day of exploring.

Activities Suited for Late Afternoon:

- Leisurely walks around balanced rocks or along park avenues where the setting sun casts long shadows.

- Sunset photography sessions at viewpoints like Dead Horse Point or Canyonlands' Grand View Point.

By planning your visits according to these time of day strategies, you can optimize your experience in terms of lighting, temperature, and crowd levels, making your trip to Moab's natural attractions more enjoyable and fulfilling.

CHAPTER 5

Accommodations

Choosing the right accommodation is crucial to the success of any trip, especially when visiting areas with attractions as popular as Arches National Park and the surrounding Moab region. The options available range from rustic campgrounds to luxury resorts, each offering different experiences and amenities that can cater to the unique needs of every traveler. This chapter focuses on helping you select the best place to stay during your visit, considering factors such as proximity to attractions, type of accommodation, budget, and the kind of experience you are seeking.

Whether you are a solo adventurer looking for a simple base camp to recharge between hikes, a family needing comfortable amenities and easy access to tourist sites, or a couple on a romantic getaway seeking upscale lodging and privacy, there is something in Moab and its environs for everyone. We will explore a variety of lodging options, from hotels and motels in the heart of Moab to secluded cabins and upscale resorts a little further afield. We'll also discuss seasonal considerations, the advantages of different locations, and tips on booking the best accommodation based on your itinerary.

Understanding the pros and cons of various accommodations will enable you to make informed decisions that enhance your overall trip experience, ensuring that each day ends as wonderfully as it begins.

Where to Stay

When visiting Arches National Park, choosing the right accommodation can greatly influence your overall experience. Whether you prefer avoiding crowded hotels or seeking a unique stay that enhances your connection with nature, Moab and its surrounding areas offer a range of options that cater to different preferences and budgets.

Options for Avoiding Crowded Hotels

For those looking to steer clear of crowded hotels, particularly during peak tourist seasons, several alternatives offer peace and a bit more exclusivity:

Boutique Hotels:

Boutique hotels in Moab provide a personalized experience with unique thematic decor and attentive service. These smaller hotels often offer a quiet retreat after a day of exploring. Examples include the Gonzo Inn, with its eclectic, artsy vibe, and the Moab Springs Ranch, which combines luxury with environmental consciousness.

Vacation Rentals:

Renting a vacation home or apartment can provide a more private and homely environment. Platforms like Airbnb or Vrbo have numerous listings in and around Moab, from modern apartments in downtown Moab to secluded houses near the parks. These accommodations often come with the added benefits of full kitchens and private outdoor spaces.

Bed and Breakfasts:

For a cozy, intimate lodging experience, consider staying at a bed and breakfast. These establishments offer a warm, personal touch and are usually run by locals who provide invaluable insight into the area. Cali Cochitta and Sunflower Hill Luxury Inn are well-known for their charming atmospheres and homemade breakfasts.

Recommendations for Unique Stays (Cabins, Campgrounds, etc.)

For those looking to immerse themselves fully in the natural beauty of the Utah landscape, here are some recommendations for unique stays that provide more than just a place to sleep:

Cabins:

- Staying in a cabin can provide a rustic yet comfortable experience. Moab KOA offers cabins that range from basic (with just beds) to deluxe (with private bathrooms and kitchens). These can be a great middle ground between camping and hotels.

- Castle Valley Inn, located about 30 minutes from Moab, offers secluded cabins with stunning views of red rock cliffs and acres of natural gardens.

Campgrounds:

- Camping is a fantastic way to connect with the outdoors. The Devils Garden Campground inside Arches National Park offers sites amid spectacular rock formations, though reservations are required well in advance due to its popularity.

- Outside the park, ACT Campground provides an eco-friendly camping experience with options for tent sites, RV spots, and even small cabin-like rooms.

Glamping:

- For those who like the idea of camping but prefer the comforts of a bed and other amenities, glamping (glamorous camping) is a perfect choice. Under Canvas Moab offers luxury tent accommodations with comfortable beds, en suite bathrooms, and daily housekeeping, all set against the backdrop of stunning natural scenery.

Unique and Offbeat:

- For a truly unique experience, consider staying in offbeat accommodations like the yurts at Dead Horse Point State Park or the Conestoga wagons at Capitol Reef Resort. These accommodations combine the pioneer spirit with modern comforts.

These accommodations provide a place to rest and enhance your experience by keeping you close to nature or offering a distinctive local flavor. Whether you choose the independence of a vacation rental, the rustic charm of a cabin, the community aspect of a campground, or the chic experience of glamping, each option offers a different way to enjoy the spectacular environment of the Arches National Park area.

Booking Strategies

Finding the perfect place to stay near popular destinations like Arches National Park can be a daunting task, especially when most tourists flock towards the most advertised options. Here are some effective strategies to discover less popular, yet charming lodging options that may offer a quieter, more personalized experience away from the mainstream.

How to Find Less Popular Lodging Options

Utilize Local Resources:

- **Contact Local Visitor Centers:** Often, local visitor centers have knowledge of quaint, lesser-known accommodations such as family-run inns, boutique motels, or cabins that aren't heavily advertised.

- **Engage with Local Forums or Social Media Groups:** Platforms like TripAdvisor forums or Facebook community groups dedicated to Moab or Utah travel can provide personal recommendations and insider tips on where to stay away from the usual tourist spots.

Explore Niche Booking Websites:

- **Specialty Sites:** Look beyond the large booking platforms and explore websites that specialize in unique or boutique accommodations. For example, *Glamping Hub* focuses on luxurious camping experiences, while *BoutiqueHomes* offers a selection of individually styled homes and hotels.

- **Agritourism Sites:** Websites like *Farm Stay U.S.* can lead you to lodging on working farms and ranches, which might offer a completely different perspective of the Moab region.

Expand Your Search Radius:

- **Look Beyond Moab:** Consider staying in less frequented towns such as Green River, Monticello, or even Blanding. These places are within a reasonable driving distance to the parks but are typically less crowded and might offer more competitive pricing.

- **Investigate Surrounding Areas:** Sometimes, properties located a bit off the main tourist paths provide reduced rates and unique local experiences.

Check Smaller, Independent Properties:

- **Boutique Hotels and B&Bs:** Small hotels and bed and breakfasts often provide a cozy atmosphere that larger hotels can't match. They might not appear on major travel sites but can be found through local business directories or by direct inquiries.

- **Vacation Rentals:** Properties listed on Airbnb, Vrbo, or other vacation rental sites might be located in quieter neighborhoods or offer unique amenities like kitchen facilities or private yards.

Use Technology to Your Advantage:

- **Google Maps:** Search for accommodations via Google Maps to uncover smaller establishments that don't rank on the first page of traditional travel search engines.

- **Mobile Apps:** Apps like *HotelTonight* can offer last-minute deals on hotels and often feature smaller boutique options that aren't fully booked.

Plan and Book Early:

- **Avoid Peak Times:** Booking well in advance allows you to choose from the best options before they fill up, especially during peak tourist seasons.

- **Flexible Dates:** If your schedule allows, try to visit during shoulder seasons or mid-week when demand is lower. Accommodations are cheaper and less crowded.

Direct Contact:

- **Call Directly:** Once you find a property you are interested in, call them directly for a booking. Some smaller lodges and B&Bs reserve their best rooms or rates for clients who book directly, and it also allows you to ask detailed questions about the property and surroundings.

Using these strategies will help you find accommodations that may offer a more authentic and peaceful experience but also allow you to explore the Moab area in a more relaxed and enjoyable way. By stepping off the beaten path, you can uncover hidden gems that make your visit truly memorable.

CHAPTER 6

Transportation Tips

Navigating the logistics of transportation is crucial to ensuring a smooth and stress-free vacation, especially in areas like Moab and Arches National Park, where attractions are spread out across vast landscapes. Efficiently planning how to get around maximizes your time and enhances your overall travel experience by minimizing delays and complications. This chapter delves into the various transportation options available in the Moab area, offering practical advice on how to choose the best mode of transport based on your itinerary, budget, and personal travel preferences.

Whether you're flying into the region, renting a car, considering public transportation, or exploring bike rentals, understanding your options and planning accordingly can make a significant difference. We will cover tips for everything from navigating local roads to making the most of shuttle services within the parks. Additionally, for those looking to reduce their environmental impact, we'll explore eco-friendly transportation choices that are both practical and sustainable.

By the end of this chapter, you should have a comprehensive understanding of the transportation dynamics in the Moab region, equipped with the knowledge to navigate the area efficiently, safely, and enjoyably. This guidance aims to ensure that your travel logistics complement your adventure, allowing you to focus on the breathtaking landscapes and unforgettable experiences that await you.

Getting There

Traveling to Moab, Utah, home to some of the most stunning natural landscapes in the United States requires some planning to ensure a smooth journey. Whether you're coming to explore Arches National Park, Canyonlands National Park, or the surrounding wilderness, knowing the best routes and travel strategies is essential.

Best Travel Routes to Avoid Busy Roads

When planning your trip to Moab, considering the time of year and day can greatly affect your driving experience due to seasonal traffic peaks and routine congestion near popular sites.

From Northern Utah or Salt Lake City:

- Take Interstate 15 S to US-6 E towards Price. This route is generally less congested compared to other highways and offers scenic views as you approach the Moab area. Continue on US-191 S, which will take you directly into Moab.

- **Alternative Route:** For a more scenic and potentially less trafficked journey, consider taking the slightly longer route via US-40 E through Vernal, then south through Dinosaur National Monument and down to Moab via US-191 S. This detour avoids the busier I-70 corridor and adds stunning geological features and dinosaur excavation sites to your trip.

From Southern Utah or Arizona:

- If you are traveling from southern Utah or coming from Arizona, US-191 N provides a direct route to Moab. This road is less busy outside of peak tourist seasons in the spring and fall.

- **Scenic Detour:** Take US-163 N to US-191 N to incorporate a visit to Monument Valley or the Four Corners Monument. This route offers breathtaking views and a quieter drive, which is especially beneficial during off-peak travel times.

Avoiding Traffic:

- Plan to drive during early morning hours or late afternoons during weekdays to avoid the highest traffic volumes, especially near park entrances and in downtown Moab.

- Check local travel advisories for any seasonal road works or events that might affect traffic, and always have a backup route planned.

Suggested Airports and Car Rental Tips

Airports:

- **Grand Junction Regional Airport (GJT):** Located about 110 miles north of Moab, GJT offers the closest commercial flights with connections to major cities. Car rentals are available at the airport, making it a convenient option for most travelers.

- **Salt Lake City International Airport (SLC):** While further away, about 230 miles from Moab, SLC offers a wider range of flights and sometimes more competitive prices. Renting a car from here gives you the freedom to explore several scenic routes to Moab.

Car Rental Tips:

- **Book Early:** Car rental demand in Utah can be high, especially during peak tourist seasons. Booking your vehicle well in advance ensures availability and often secures a better rate.

- **Consider Your Needs:** Depending on the activities planned, consider the type of vehicle you rent. A standard car is suitable for most travel, but a high-clearance or 4WD vehicle might be necessary if you plan to explore rugged backcountry roads or remote areas within the parks.

- **Insurance:** Check whether your car insurance covers rental cars or if you need to purchase additional coverage from the rental company. This can save you money and give you peace of mind.

- **Pickup/Drop-off:** If possible, try to arrange your car pickup and drop-off at the same location to avoid additional fees. If you're not from the area, familiarize yourself with the local driving laws and regulations.

By planning your route carefully and understanding your transportation options, you can start your Moab adventure stress-free and ready to explore the region's incredible natural beauty.

Navigating the Area

Exploring the Moab region and its iconic national parks involves more than just hitting the main attractions. Knowing how to navigate the area effectively can significantly enhance your experience. From scenic drives that showcase the breathtaking landscape to tips for venturing off the beaten path, this section will guide you on how to make the most of your travels in this stunning part of Utah.

Recommended Scenic Drives and Backroads

Moab is surrounded by an expansive natural playground that offers some of the most scenic drives in the United States. Here are a few must-do routes:

Scenic Byway 128:

Known as the River Road, this route follows the Colorado River from Moab to Cisco. It's lined with towering red rock cliffs and provides numerous pull-offs for photography. This road is less traveled than the main park roads and offers access to several lesser-known trails and river access points.

La Sal Mountain Loop Road:

This drive combines forested mountains with desert landscapes, providing a complete contrast to the red rock scenery around Moab. The loop takes you into the La Sal Mountains, offering cooling temperatures during summer and spectacular views of the surrounding desert below.

Potash Road (SR-279):

Starting just north of Moab, this drive skirts along the Colorado River to Potash. It's particularly famous for its rock art panels and dinosaur tracks. The road is less crowded and offers stunning views of sheer cliff walls and ancient petroglyphs.

Shafer Trail:

For those with a high-clearance vehicle, the Shafer Trail offers an unforgettable off-road experience. Starting from the Island in the Sky district of Canyonlands, this road descends via switchbacks to the valley floor, providing breathtaking views and a thrilling drive.

Gemini Bridges Road:

This backcountry route is accessible via a dirt road suitable for most vehicles under dry conditions. It leads to the Gemini

Bridges, a pair of natural arches that are a highlight of the lesser-visited attractions near Moab.

Tips for Exploring Off the Beaten Path

Venturing off the beaten path in the Moab area allows for more intimate experiences with nature and the chance to see parts of the landscape that few visitors explore. Here are some tips to safely and responsibly explore these areas:

Prepare Your Vehicle:

If you plan to explore backroads, ensure your vehicle is suitable for off-road conditions. A high-clearance, 4WD vehicle is often necessary for many of Moab's dirt roads. Always carry spare tires, extra water, and emergency supplies.

Respect the Environment:

Stick to designated roads and trails to minimize your impact on the fragile desert ecosystem. The cryptobiotic soil crust is vital for preventing erosion but is easily damaged.

Plan Your Route:

Always have a detailed map or GPS when venturing off the main roads. Cell service can be spotty or nonexistent in remote areas, making navigation challenging.

Check Local Conditions:

Road conditions can vary widely depending on the weather. Check with local ranger stations or visitor centers for the latest information on road closures and conditions, especially after rain or snow.

Carry Sufficient Supplies:

When exploring remote areas, bring enough water, food, and sun protection. Weather conditions can change rapidly, so also pack appropriate clothing.

Inform Someone of Your Plans:

Always let someone know your planned route and expected return time, especially when heading into less frequented areas.

By following these scenic drives and backroad adventures, you'll discover the hidden beauties of Moab that many visitors miss. Remember, the key to enjoying these off-the-beaten-path experiences is preparation and respect for the natural environment, ensuring these areas remain pristine for years to come.

CHAPTER 7

Activities and Experiences

Moab, Utah, is a treasure trove of outdoor adventures, cultural experiences, and breathtaking landscapes that cater to a wide range of interests and ability levels. From the rugged trails of Arches National Park to the vast expanses of Canyonlands, the region offers more than just sightseeing—it invites visitors to engage actively with their environment.

With a landscape as varied and dramatic as Moab's, the potential for memorable experiences is boundless. Whether you are a seasoned outdoor enthusiast or a family looking for a mix of activities suitable for all ages, Moab delivers a natural playground that is both accessible and awe-inspiring. This chapter aims to guide you through planning a trip filled with exciting, enriching activities that will leave you with lasting impressions of this unique corner of the world.

Outdoor Adventures

Moab is not just a destination; it's an invitation to adventure. The region's red rock landscapes and rugged terrains offer endless opportunities for outdoor enthusiasts. From serene hikes on less-trodden paths to adrenaline-pumping activities like canyoneering, Moab caters to every level of adventure seeker. This section will explore some of the best outdoor adventures in Moab, focusing on less frequented hiking trails and alternative activities that provide unique ways to experience the area's natural beauty.

Hiking Trails That Are Less Frequented

While the popular trails in Arches and Canyonlands National Parks often see high foot traffic, several lesser-known trails offer equally stunning scenery without the crowds:

Syncline Loop (Canyonlands National Park - Island in the Sky):

This challenging 8.3-mile loop circles Upheaval Dome and offers solitude along with rigorous hiking through varied terrain. The trail descends into the syncline, where hikers can experience the raw, untouched landscapes of Canyonlands.

Fisher Towers Trail:

Located about 20 miles northeast of Moab, this 4.4-mile trail offers one of the area's most striking settings. The trail weaves through dramatic red rock towers and spires, which are popular among photographers and climbers. Despite its beauty, Fisher Towers typically sees fewer visitors than the national parks.

Hidden Valley Trail:

A 4-mile out-and-back trail that leads to a lush hidden valley bordered by Navajo sandstone cliffs. After an initial steep hike, the trail flattens out, offering peaceful walking conditions and spectacular views of the Moab Valley.

Stairmaster Trail (Canyonlands - The Maze):

For the ultimate in solitude and unmarked trails, the Stairmaster in The Maze district is perfect for experienced hikers seeking isolation and adventure. This area requires preparation and possibly a guide, as it involves navigating a remote and challenging landscape.

Alternative Activities (e.g., Canyoneering, Stargazing)

For those looking for something different from traditional hiking, Moab offers a plethora of alternative activities:

Canyoneering:

Moab is renowned for its canyoneering opportunities. This activity combines hiking, rappelling, and sometimes swimming, allowing adventurers to explore the spectacular slot canyons that are not accessible by regular trails. Companies like Moab Cliffs and Canyons offer guided tours that cater to all skill levels.

Stargazing:

Moab's remote location away from city lights makes it an ideal spot for stargazing. Arches National Park, a designated International Dark Sky Park, offers nighttime programs and stargazing events. The park's Panorama Point is a popular spot for setting up telescopes and enjoying the night sky.

Mountain Biking:

The Moab area boasts some of the world's best mountain biking trails. Routes like the Slickrock Trail are internationally famous, but other less-known trails, such as Klondike Bluffs and the Moab Brand Trails, offer fantastic rides with fewer crowds.

River Rafting:

The Colorado River provides excellent opportunities for whitewater rafting with a range of rapids that cater to beginners as well as seasoned rafters. Guided rafting trips can offer a thrilling way to see the landscape from a different perspective.

Rock Climbing:

With its abundant sandstone cliffs, Moab is a climber's paradise. Areas like Wall Street, a roadside cliff along the Potash Road, are popular, but there are numerous other spots that provide a wide variety of routes and challenges.

By engaging in these less frequented hikes and alternative activities, visitors can truly immerse themselves in the unique environment that Moab offers, enjoying the outdoors away from the main tourist paths and discovering a more personal connection with nature.

Cultural Experiences

Moab and its surrounding areas are a hotspot for outdoor adventures and a region rich in cultural history and community spirit. Engaging with local communities and exploring the small towns and attractions offer visitors a deeper understanding and appreciation of the area.

Engaging with Local Communities

Connecting with local communities in Moab and the surrounding area can enrich your visit by providing insights into the region's history, traditions, and current way of life. Here's how you can engage meaningfully with the locals:

Participate in Local Events and Festivals:

- Moab hosts several annual events that reflect the area's vibrant community spirit and cultural heritage. The Moab Music Festival, for instance, offers a series of concerts featuring diverse music genres set against the breathtaking backdrop of red rock landscapes. The Moab Folk Festival is another great event that showcases folk music, local art, and craft.

- Participating in these events supports local artists and businesses and provides an opportunity to mingle with residents and experience the local culture firsthand.

Volunteer Opportunities:

- Volunteering can be a powerful way to connect with the community. Organizations like the Plateau Restoration and Conservation Adventures offer opportunities to help with environmental conservation projects. This can be a rewarding experience that allows you to contribute positively while learning about the local ecosystem.

Shop at Local Markets:

- Visit the Moab Farmers Market, which runs from spring to fall. Here, you can buy locally grown produce, handmade crafts, and unique artworks while interacting with local farmers and artisans. This is an excellent way to support the local economy and take home a piece of Moab.

Cultural Workshops and Tours:

- Look for workshops or tours that focus on local crafts, cuisine, or history. These activities often provide a more intimate look at the local culture and traditions. For example, some tours, guided by local experts, offer insights into Native American history and rock art in the area.

Visiting Small Towns and Local Attractions

Exploring small towns around Moab provides a glimpse into the area's history and charm that you might miss if you stick only to the well-trodden paths.

Bluff:

A small town with a rich history, Bluff is home to fascinating historical sites like the Bluff Fort Historic Site, which tells the story of early Mormon settlers in the area. The town is also a gateway to some of the most impressive ancient Native American rock art and ruins in the region.

Castle Valley:

Located about 16 miles northeast of Moab, Castle Valley offers picturesque views of towering red rock formations. The town itself is small but provides a peaceful escape from the busier Moab area. It's also a popular spot for filmmakers, providing a fun backdrop for movie buffs.

Green River:

About 45 minutes northwest of Moab, Green River offers a slice of Americana with its historic downtown, melon farms, and the John Wesley Powell River History Museum. The museum provides an excellent overview of Powell's explorations and the history of river running in the American West.

Local Wineries and Breweries:

Visiting local wineries and breweries, such as the Castle Creek Winery in Moab, offers a taste of local flavors and an understanding of the area's agricultural and entrepreneurial spirit. Most establishments offer tours and tastings, allowing you to enjoy local produce in a scenic setting.

By engaging with local communities and exploring small towns and local attractions, visitors can experience a side of Moab that goes beyond its famous landscapes, enriching their trip with cultural depth and personal interactions. This approach supports the local economy and promotes a sustainable tourism model that benefits both visitors and residents.

Stargazing Opportunities

Moab, with its expansive desert skies, is a haven for stargazers. The lack of light pollution in the remote areas surrounding Moab and its national parks provides prime conditions for night sky viewing. This section will explore the best practices for stargazing, focusing on how to enjoy this celestial spectacle in less crowded spots, ensuring a serene and unforgettable experience.

Tips for Enjoying the Night Sky in Less Crowded Spots

Choosing the Right Location:

- **Away from City Lights:** To maximize the clarity of the night sky, choose locations that are as far removed from city lights as possible. Areas like Canyonlands National

Park's Island in the Sky and The Needles provide some of the darkest skies in the region.

- **Accessible but Remote:** Look for spots that are accessible by car or a short hike but are still off the beaten path. The Gemini Bridges road, for example, offers a less frequented route with areas where you can pull off and set up for an evening under the stars.

Timing Your Stargazing:

- **Moon Phases:** The best time for stargazing is during the new moon when the sky is darkest. Avoid times around the full moon, as the moonlight can wash out the fainter stars.

- **Meteor Showers and Astronomical Events:** Plan your stargazing around known meteor showers and other celestial events for a more dramatic experience. Check an astronomical calendar for the best dates.

Equipment and Preparation:

- **Use of Red Flashlights:** To preserve your night vision, use red lights instead of standard flashlights or your phone's flashlight. Red light has a longer wavelength and does not disrupt your ability to see the stars.

- **Binoculars and Telescopes:** While much of the Milky Way can be seen with the naked eye, binoculars or a small telescope can enhance your viewing experience, allowing you to see more detail.

- **Comfort and Safety:** Bring warm clothing, blankets, and perhaps a reclining chair or a blanket to lie on. Nights in the desert can be cold, even in summer. Ensure you have plenty of water and snacks, and always let someone know where you will be, especially if venturing into more remote areas.

Photographing the Night Sky:

- **Camera Settings:** To photograph the night sky, use a DSLR camera with manual mode capability. Set your lens to its widest aperture, use a high ISO setting, and use long exposure times. A tripod is essential to keep your camera stable and capture clear, sharp images.

- **Using a Star Tracker:** For serious astrophotography, consider using a star tracker. This device moves your camera in alignment with the Earth's rotation, allowing for longer exposures without star trails.

Educational Opportunities:

- **Join a Guided Star Party:** Check if there are any guided stargazing tours or "star parties" during your visit.

Rangers and astronomers often host these events, providing telescopes and sharing knowledge about constellations, planets, and deep-sky objects.

- **Apps and Star Charts:** Use apps like Star Walk, SkyView, or Stellarium to help identify stars, planets, and constellations. These can enhance your knowledge and enjoyment of the stargazing experience.

By following these tips and embracing the remote, dark skies of Moab and its surroundings, you can enjoy one of the most profound and beautiful natural spectacles on Earth. Stargazing in this region offers a chance to witness the wonders of the universe and provides a peaceful escape into the tranquility of nature at night.

CHAPTER 8

Food and Dining

Moab, Utah, is a gateway to some of the most iconic national parks in the United States and a vibrant hub for diverse and delicious dining options. This chapter delves into Moab's culinary scene, exploring everything from cozy cafes and gourmet restaurants to local diners and food trucks.

Moab's culinary landscape is as varied as its geological one, offering an array of flavors that can enhance your stay. From southwestern flavors that reflect the area's cultural heritage to innovative cuisine that showcases modern culinary trends, Moab is sure to impress.

Eating Off the Beaten Path

When visiting a popular destination like Moab, it's often the small, hidden gems that make dining memorable. Beyond the main drag and well-known eateries, there are countless opportunities to enjoy good food away from the crowds. In this section, we explore less frequented local spots and offer tips for those who prefer to savor their meals surrounded by nature.

Local Eateries That Are Crowd-Free

Peace Tree Juice Café:

Nestled just off the main street, Peace Tree is known for its health-conscious menu, including fresh juices, smoothies, and hearty breakfasts. It's a great spot to enjoy a relaxing meal away from the bustling tourist areas.

Milt's Stop & Eat:

Moab's oldest restaurant offers a nostalgic dining experience. Its menu includes burgers, fries, and shakes made from locally sourced ingredients. Located slightly away from the center, Milt's sees fewer tourists and more locals.

Desert Bistro:

For a quieter, more upscale dining experience, Desert Bistro offers a tranquil patio and a menu that creatively uses local ingredients. It's the perfect place for a peaceful dinner after a day of hiking.

Quesadilla Mobilla:

Off the main roads, this local food truck serves up gourmet quesadillas with a unique twist. It's usually parked in a less crowded area, making it a great stop for grabbing a quick, delicious, and crowd-free meal.

La Sal House:

Situated a bit off the beaten path, La Sal House offers a cozy ambiance with a menu that highlights local produce and meats. Their dishes are inspired by the Southwest but have a modern flair, making each meal a culinary adventure.

Tips for Picnicking and Cooking Outdoors

Picnicking and cooking outdoors can enrich your connection with Moab's natural beauty. Here are some tips to make the most of dining al fresco in the great outdoors:

Choose the Right Spot:

- **Scenic Locations:** Choose a location that allows picnicking and offers breathtaking views. The banks along the Colorado River, as do areas around Fisher Towers and Dead Horse Point State Park, provide numerous spots.

- **Shade and Shelter:** Especially in the summer months, choose spots with natural shade or bring your own sun shelter to stay comfortable.

Prepare Properly:

- **Packing Essentials:** Bring a durable, lightweight blanket or a portable table and chairs. Include all necessary utensils, reusable plates, and cups to minimize waste.

- **Coolers:** Invest in a good cooler to keep perishable items fresh, especially if you plan to spend the whole day out or if you're cooking perishable foods.

Cooking Outdoors:

- **Portable Cookware:** If open fires are not allowed, use portable stoves or grills. Always check fire regulations in the area, as they can change with weather conditions.

- **Simple Recipes:** Choose simple recipes that require minimal cooking but are nutritious and satisfying. Consider premade salads, sandwiches, or quick-cook items like hot dogs and burgers.

Leave No Trace:

- **Clean Up:** Always pack out what you brought in, including all garbage, leftover food, and litter. Leave your picnic or cooking site cleaner than you found it to help preserve Moab's natural beauty.

- **Wildlife Safety:** Keep all food secured and dispose of waste properly to avoid attracting wildlife.

Eating off the beaten path in Moab offers a delightful break from the typical tourist experiences, allowing you to enjoy unique flavors and stunning landscapes. Whether you choose to dine at a secluded local eatery or amidst the breathtaking scenery, these experiences will add an unforgettable flavor to your adventure.

Farmers' Markets and Local Produce

In a region as naturally diverse as Moab, the availability of fresh, local produce and handcrafted goods offers a unique culinary exploration that complements the scenic backdrop. Farmers' markets and local producers provide access to fresh ingredients and allow visitors to engage with the community and experience the area's agricultural bounty away from the typical tourist routes. This section delves into how to find and enjoy these local treasures.

Finding Fresh, Local Food While Avoiding Tourist Traps

Explore Local Farmers' Markets:

- **Moab Farmers' Market:** This is a key spot to enjoy local produce and crafts. Held weekly from spring to fall, it features vendors selling everything from fresh fruits and vegetables to artisan breads and local honey. It's a fantastic place to mingle with locals and enjoy the community vibe.

- **Tips for Visiting:** Arrive early for the best selection. Many vendors sell out quickly, especially popular items like organic vegetables and homemade jams. Bring cash, though some vendors may accept cards, and don't forget reusable bags for your purchases.

Visit Local Farms:

- **Youth Garden Project:** A non-profit community garden that offers produce and a chance to learn about sustainable gardening in a desert environment. They sometimes host community events and dinners, which can provide a delicious educational experience.

- **Castle Valley Farms:** Known for its orchards and vineyards, Castle Valley Farms offers tours and direct sales of its produce. Visiting a farm can give you insight into the farming challenges and innovations in Utah's arid landscape.

Utilize Farm Stands and Co-ops:

- **Moab Co-op:** A local initiative that brings together produce from several smaller farms in the area. Shopping at the co-op is a great way to get a variety of items in one place, supporting a range of local growers.

- **Roadside Stands:** Look for roadside stands, especially when driving through rural areas outside Moab. These stands often sell fresh produce straight from the garden or orchard.

Check Out Specialty Stores:

- **Moonflower Community Cooperative:** Although not a farmers' market, Moonflower is a local grocery that emphasizes organic and local products from vegetables and fruits to local meats and dairy. It's a great spot to grab ingredients for a picnic or a home-cooked meal.

- **Local Butchers and Bakers:** For those looking to cook their own meals, visiting local butchers can provide access to high-quality, locally-sourced meats. Local bakeries offer breads and pastries baked fresh daily, perfect for a quick snack or a morning treat.

Dining at Farm-to-Table Restaurants:

- **The Farm Bistro:** Offers meals prepared with local ingredients, showcasing the flavors of the season in a menu that changes based on what's available locally.

- **98 Center Moab:** While not strictly farm-to-table, this restaurant uses local produce to enhance their Asian-inspired menu, offering fresh, vibrant dishes.

Engage with Local Food Events:

- **Culinary Festivals:** Participate in local food festivals or special dining events hosted by restaurants featuring local products. These events often promote sustainable agriculture and celebrate the region's culinary diversity.

By actively seeking out farmers' markets, local produce, and community-oriented food events, you enjoy fresh, delicious ingredients and contribute to the local economy, making your visit more sustainable and connected to the region. These experiences allow you to taste the true flavor of Moab while avoiding the more commercialized and tourist-oriented spots.

CHAPTER 9

Safety and Preparedness

Exploring the stunning landscapes and vast wilderness areas around Moab, Utah, requires more than just a sense of adventure—it demands a strong commitment to safety and preparedness. Safety and preparedness are the foundations of any successful outdoor activity, especially in areas as challenging and isolated as those around Moab. By being well-prepared and informed, you can enjoy the breathtaking beauty of this region with confidence and peace of mind.

Staying Safe in Less Crowded Areas

Exploring the less crowded, remote areas around Moab offers a unique adventure but also requires a heightened level of safety awareness and preparation. While solitude is part of these areas' allure, it also means fewer immediate resources and help in case of an emergency.

Tips for Wilderness Safety and Navigation

Plan and Prepare:

- **Research Your Destination:** Before heading out, research the area you plan to explore. Understand the terrain, typical weather conditions, and any potential hazards you might encounter.

- **Leave an Itinerary:** Always leave a detailed itinerary with someone you trust. Include your planned route, expected return time, and contact information.

Navigation Skills:

- **Use Reliable Maps and GPS:** Carry a detailed map of the area and a GPS device. While mobile phones can serve as GPS devices, do not rely solely on them, as battery life is limited and service may be unavailable.

- **Learn Basic Navigation:** Familiarize yourself with basic navigation skills using a compass and map. Knowing how to orient yourself in remote areas can be lifesaving.

Carry Essential Gear:

- **The Ten Essentials:** Always pack the Ten Essentials for outdoor activities, which include navigation tools, sun protection, extra clothing, a flashlight, first-aid supplies, fire starters, repair tools, extra food, water, and emergency shelter.

- **Appropriate Clothing:** Wear appropriate clothing and sturdy footwear. Layering is key in desert environments where temperatures can fluctuate dramatically.

Water and Food:

- **Hydration:** Always carry more water than you think you will need. Desert conditions can lead to rapid dehydration. Consider packing a portable water filter or purification tablets as a backup.

- **Caloric Intake:** Bring high-energy, easily digestible foods to maintain your energy levels throughout the day.

Weather Awareness:

- **Check the Weather:** Always check the weather forecast before your trip. Be aware of sudden weather changes typical in desert environments, such as flash floods or thunderstorms.

- **Understand Heat and Sun Exposure:** Plan to avoid strenuous activity during the hottest part of the day, and always wear sunscreen and a hat to protect against the sun.

Wildlife Encounters:

- **Be Aware of Local Wildlife:** Know what types of wildlife you might encounter and how to interact with or avoid them safely. In Moab, this might include snakes, scorpions, or even mountain lions.

- **Secure Food and Trash:** In camping situations, secure your food and trash to prevent animals from entering your campsite.

Know Basic First Aid:

- **First Aid Kit:** Carry a well-stocked first aid kit and know how to use the items in it.

- **CPR and Emergency Procedures:** Basic knowledge of CPR and emergency procedures can be crucial, especially when traveling in groups.

Respect the Environment:

- **Follow Leave No Trace Principles:** Respect the environment by following Leave No Trace principles. This includes packing out all your trash, minimizing campfire impacts, and not disturbing wildlife or plant life.

By adhering to these safety tips and always maintaining a cautious and prepared approach, you can safely enjoy the vast, untamed wilderness areas around Moab. This careful planning and preparation allow you to immerse yourself in the natural beauty of these remote regions with confidence and respect for the natural world.

Environmental Considerations

Moab's spectacular landscapes offer adventure and demand a high level of environmental stewardship from those who come to experience its natural beauty. The delicate ecosystems, unique geology, and diverse wildlife of the area require that visitors be mindful of their impact.

Leave No Trace Principles

The Leave No Trace Center for Outdoor Ethics promotes seven core principles designed to minimize the environmental impact of outdoor activities. These principles are particularly crucial in sensitive areas like those around Moab.

<u>Plan and Prepare:</u>

Thorough preparation minimizes risks and ensures safety. This includes understanding the area's regulations, preparing for extreme weather, and ensuring you have the necessary skills and equipment for your activities.

<u>Travel and Camp on Durable Surfaces:</u>

Stick to established trails and campsites. Desert soil contains biological crusts that are very sensitive to disturbance and play a crucial role in preventing erosion and retaining moisture.

<u>Dispose of Waste Properly:</u>

Pack out all trash, leftover food, and litter. If you are in an area without amenities, use toilet facilities or carry a portable waste disposal system. Never leave human waste or toilet paper behind.

Leave What You Find:

Preserve the past: examine, but do not touch, cultural or historic structures and artifacts. Leave rocks, plants, and other natural objects as you find them.

Minimize Campfire Impacts:

Campfires can cause lasting impacts in the desert. Use a lightweight stove for cooking and enjoy a candle lantern for light. If you must have a fire, use established fire rings and keep fires small.

Respect Wildlife:

Observe wildlife from a distance. Do not follow or approach them. Never feed animals, as doing so damages their health, alters natural behaviors, and exposes them to predators and other dangers.

Be Considerate of Other Visitors:

Respect other visitors and protect the quality of their experience. Be courteous. Yield to other users on the trail and keep noise levels down in all areas.

Respecting Local Wildlife and Ecosystems

Moab's diverse habitats are home to an array of wildlife, including mammals, birds, reptiles, and insects, each playing a critical role in the ecological balance. Here's how visitors can respect and protect the local wildlife and ecosystems:

Keep Wildlife Wild:

Avoid the temptation to interact with wildlife. Feeding animals, even with what seems like harmless foods, can lead to unhealthy dependencies, illness, and even death.

Stay Informed About Endangered Species:

Educate yourself about any endangered species in the area. Understanding their challenges can help you make more informed decisions about how to behave in their habitat.

Control Pets:

Keep pets under control and on a leash, or leave them at home. Pets can chase wildlife, destroy nests, and stress the animals.

Avoid Sensitive Areas:

During certain seasons, wildlife may be more vulnerable (e.g., nesting birds during spring). If an area is designated as sensitive or off-limits, respect these boundaries to minimize disturbance.

Support Conservation Efforts:

Consider contributing to local conservation organizations that protect Moab's landscapes and wildlife. Your support can help fund important research and conservation initiatives.

By adhering to these environmental considerations, visitors can help ensure that Moab's natural beauty and ecological health are preserved for future generations.

CONCLUSION

Exploring Southern Utah and the Four Corners Area offers a unique opportunity to immerse yourself in some of the most spectacular landscapes in the United States. From the majestic formations of Arches National Park to the vast expanses of Canyonlands, the region invites adventure and contemplation alike. As we conclude this guide, let's recap the key strategies for avoiding crowds and ensuring a fulfilling and serene experience. We encourage you to explore this magnificent area at a relaxed pace.

Recap of Key Strategies for Avoiding Crowds

Timing is Everything:

Visit During Off-Peak Seasons: Early spring and late fall are less crowded. Mid-week visits also tend to attract fewer visitors than weekends.

Start Early or Stay Late: Plan to start your day at sunrise or explore during late afternoons and early evenings when most tourists have left the parks.

Choose Lesser-Known Spots:

Explore less-frequented trails and sites within the national parks and surrounding areas. Seek out hidden gems off the beaten path to enjoy solitude and untouched nature.

Be Flexible:

Monitor crowd levels and be ready to change your plans. If a popular location is overcrowded, have a backup destination in mind.

Use Alternative Entrances and Exits:

Some parks and attractions have multiple entrances. Research and use less popular ones to avoid long waits and crowded parking areas.

Research and Reserve in Advance:

Book your accommodations, campgrounds, and any required permits well in advance, especially if you plan to visit during peak tourist seasons.

Explore and Enjoy the Beauty of Southern Utah

As you set out to explore Southern Utah and the Four Corners Area, remember that the journey is as significant as the destination. Each step offers a new perspective, every path leads to discoveries, and the vast, open landscapes invite you to pause and reflect.

Embrace the Pace:

- Allow yourself the time to engage with your surroundings truly. Sit quietly beneath a towering arch, listen to the silence of the desert, watch the sunset paint the rocks with colors too numerous to name, and gaze at the stars in one of the darkest skies in North America.

Connect with Nature:

- Engage in activities that allow you to connect with the natural environment in a respectful and meaningful way. Whether it's hiking, photography, stargazing, or simply enjoying a quiet moment by the Colorado River, each experience can deepen your appreciation for this incredible region.

Learn from the Land:

- Take opportunities to learn about the geological history, cultural heritage, and ecological importance of the areas you visit. Understanding the forces that shaped these landscapes and the cultures that have thrived here can enrich your experience.

Support Local Communities:

- Support the local economies by shopping at local markets, dining at local restaurants, and participating in community events. Your contributions help sustain the communities that preserve and protect these beautiful lands.

Leave No Trace:

- Commit to leaving no trace of your visit so that future generations can also enjoy the pristine beauty of Southern Utah. Follow the guidelines for responsible travel to help preserve these natural landscapes.

Southern Utah and the Four Corners Area are places of wonder and exploration. By following these strategies, you can enjoy your travels away from the crowds, immersed in the beauty of the landscape at your own pace. Allow the red rocks, the clear skies, and the quiet solitude to rejuvenate your spirit and inspire your adventures.

Here, in the vast openness, you find the freedom to explore and the space to discover new aspects of yourself. Welcome to the heart of the American Southwest—may your journey be as breathtaking as the landscapes you are about to explore.

Made in the USA
Las Vegas, NV
10 December 2024

13790286R00193